# The Lovers

# The Lovers

Lauren Fleishman

Schilt Publishing

10/24/44

Dearest Wife:

When it comes to expressing my feelings for you, there is nothing more than I can say: "I love you with all my heart, and will continue to do so for the rest of my life. What you have done for me since our meeting has given me all the breath + strength to continue my inability to carry on with a strong

heart and steadfeast will.
Your presence always has
brought this about.

Yours forever.
Your husband.
Joe

This project was inspired by a series of love letters written by my grandfather to my grandmother during World War II that I found in a book next to his bed. The letters spoke of a young love, the type filled with expectations of a new life together. They connected me to my grandfather and his 59-year marriage in a way that I had not been able to connect to him in life. The letters inspired me to seek out and record the love stories of other long-married couples. These are the couples I met.

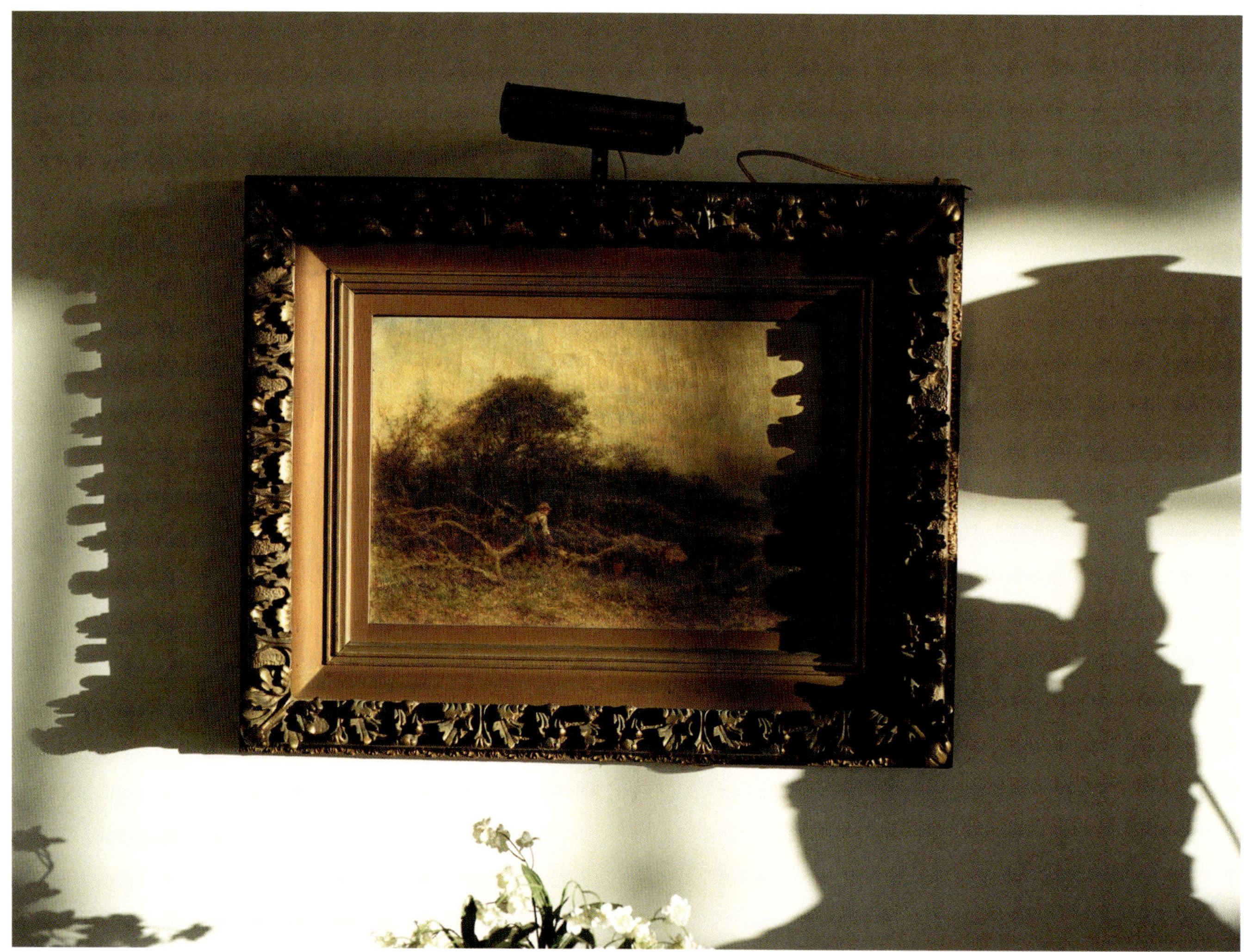

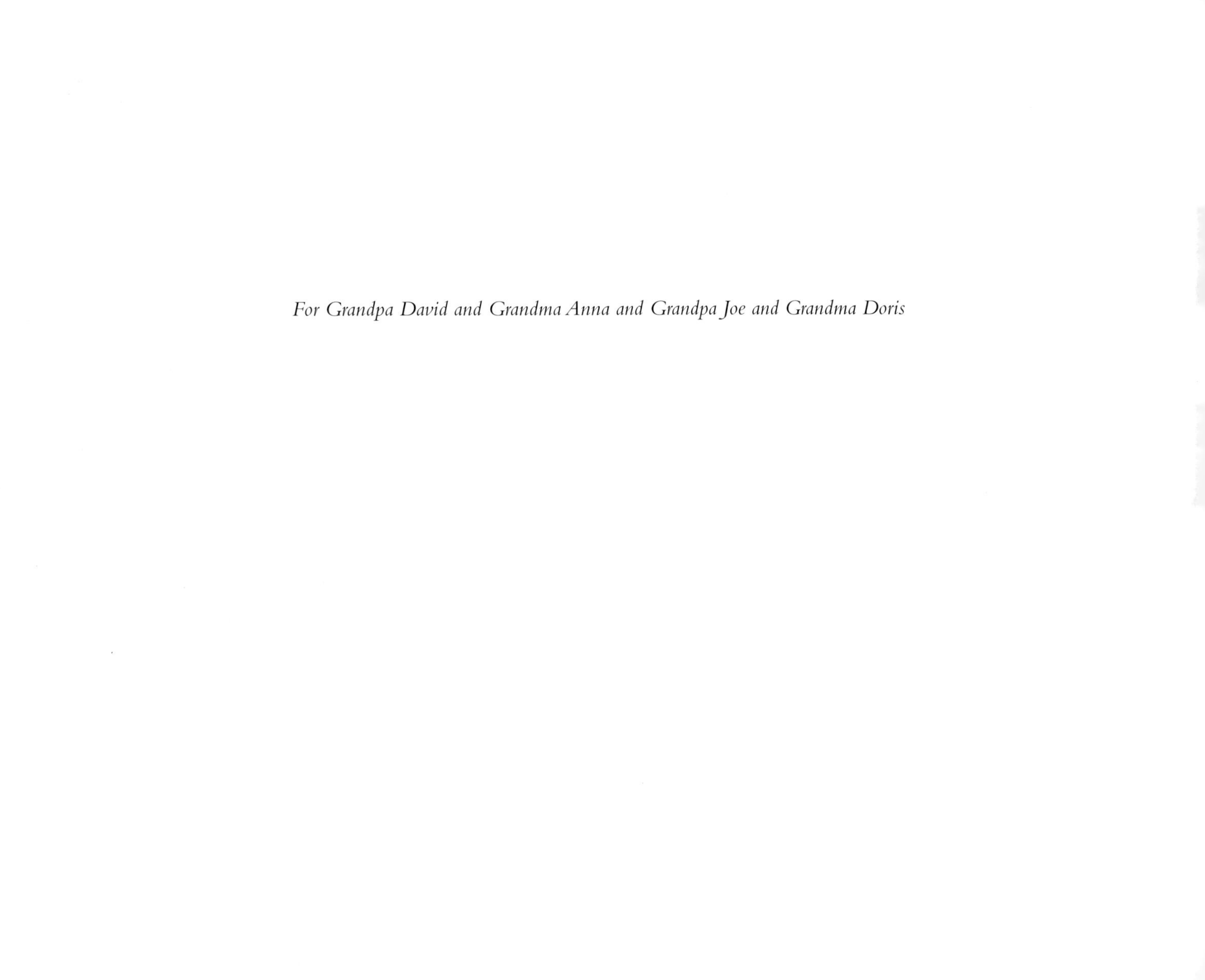

*For Grandpa David and Grandma Anna and Grandpa Joe and Grandma Doris*

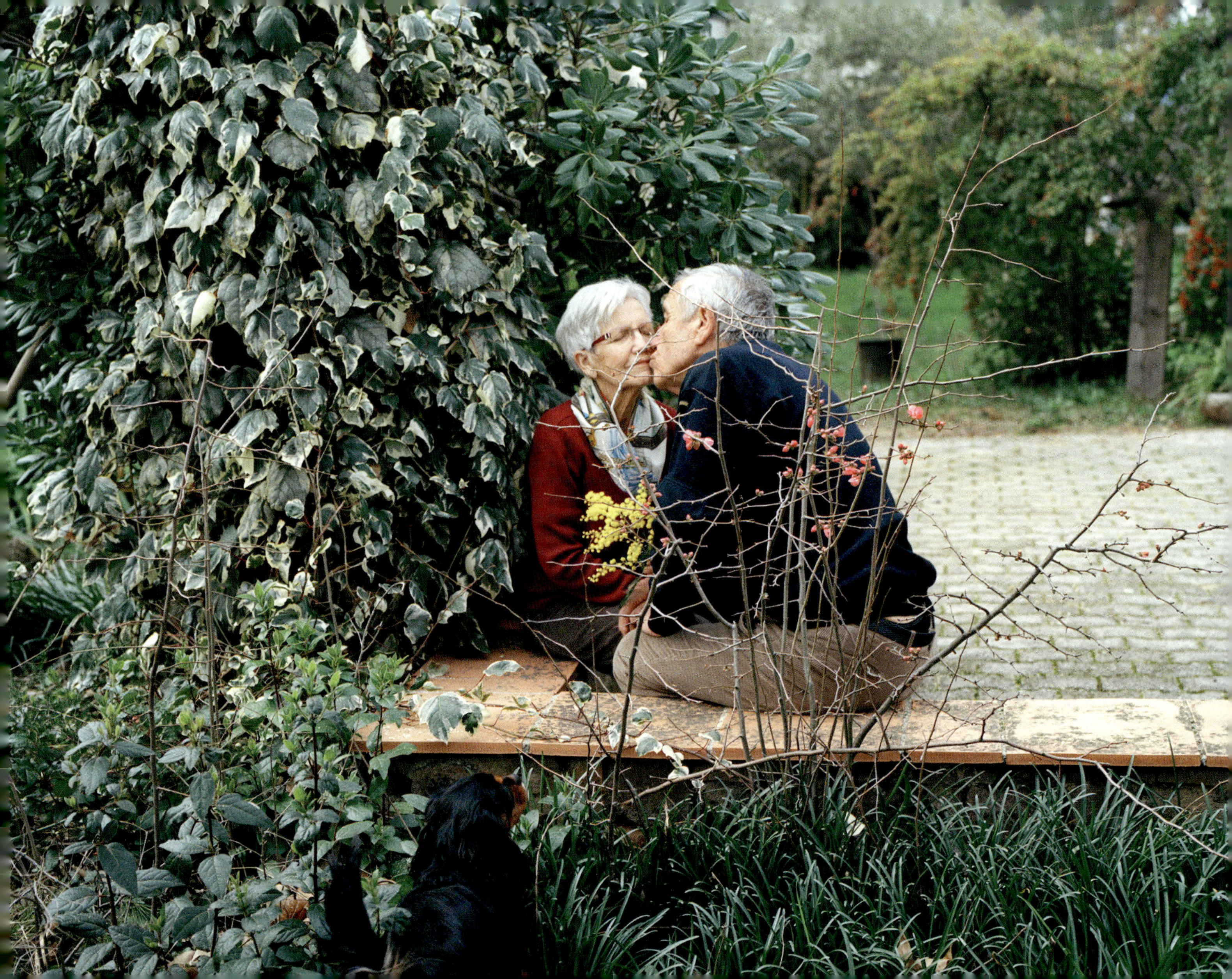

## Lucien and Fernande Einaudi

Pierrefeu-du-Var, France
Married on April 9, 1959

*Lucien* When you are young, love is completely new. It's a bit like a celebration. Then love evolves, and throughout the years you get much more attached. We were happy. We are happy. I never went looking, never had a hidden love on the side.

In marriage you acquire habits. You get used to living together, to having those habits. And after a certain age, people don't want to change anymore—they have their ways. When you continue to love each other, it's easier. For example, two days ago, I gave her flowers. It's nice! I went to go buy flowers, and I brought them to her. It was to make her happy. We are very considerate of one another. Every morning, for example, I make coffee, and I bring the coffee to her in bed. During that time she watches a bit of television. And sometimes if she stays too long in bed, I prepare breakfast—the cappuccino and everything—and I bring that to her as well.



Love is what makes life important because it's better to live with someone you love and to be loved in return than to live alone, without love. We chose to live this way because we know each other—because we can't do without one another. We need each other.

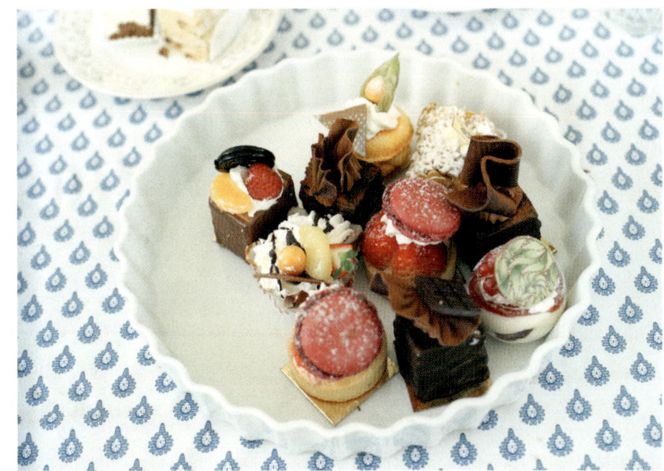

## Fred and Frances Futterman

Brooklyn, New York
Married on January 7, 1945



*Fran* My love with Fred goes back a long time. He was kind, he was friendly, he was lovable, he was amiable. As you grow older, love changes. It changes because we change. Things that were meaningful then are not as meaningful now. Not that they are meaningless but not as meaningful. I guess we have different values as time goes on.

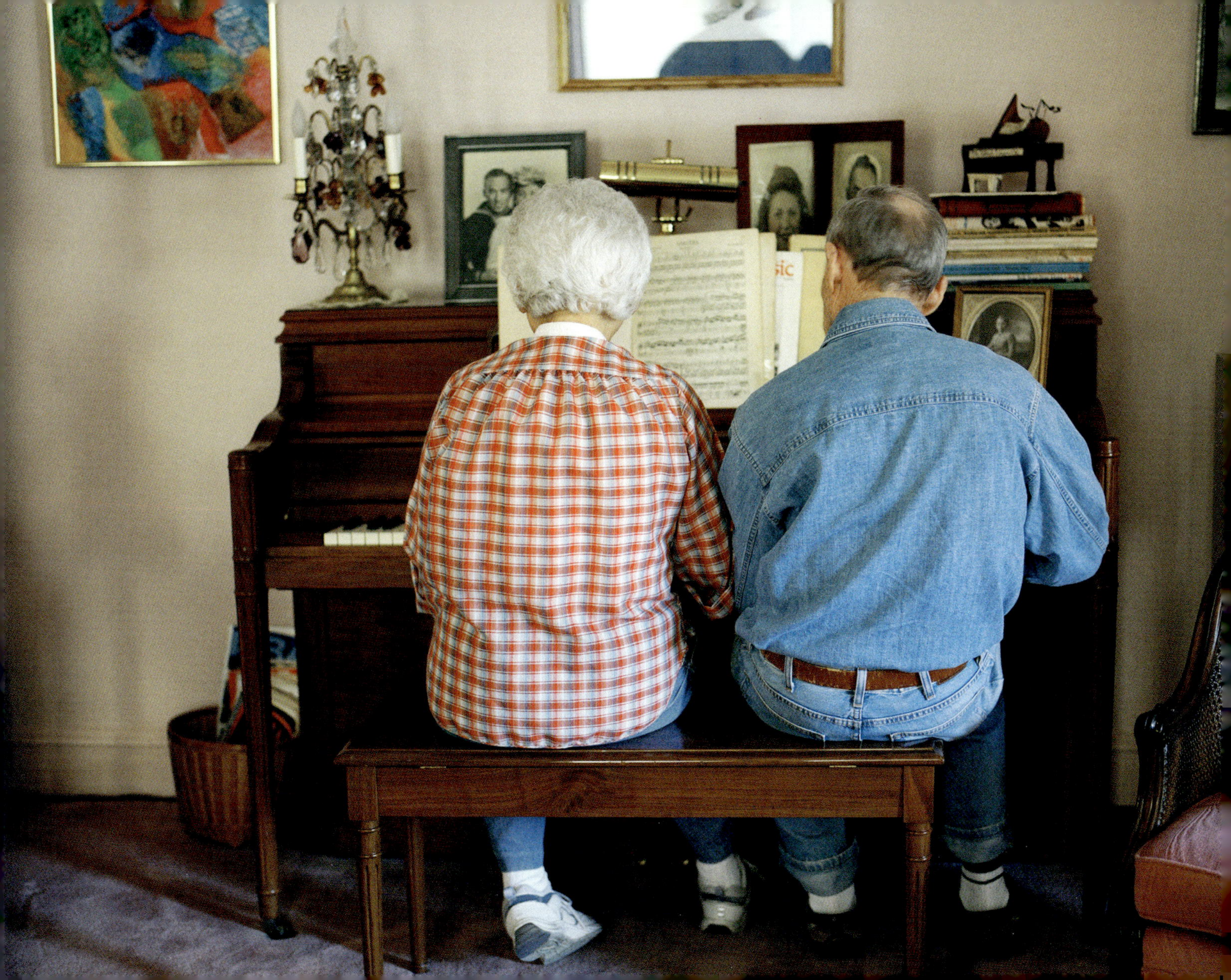

## Leon and Harriett Bolotin

Sharon, Pennsylvania
Married on November 7, 1943



*Harriett* Leon and I lead a very easy life. Leon is the type of person that believes you don't worry. This is what you do today, and if it doesn't work out, you do something else tomorrow. There's nothing you can do about it, and it's very easy. My mother was the type that whatever happened she used to wring her hands. And I would try to tell her it's so easy not to worry. But you are what you are.

*Leon* Well, the things you might worry about never happen. The roof doesn't fall in. The sky doesn't fall in. The car doesn't run off the road. It doesn't happen, so you take life as it comes. Take the easy way and worry about tomorrow tomorrow.

*Harriett* Leon and I are very compatible. We're opposites to a certain extent, but after 68 years, you meld. You just know what the other one is going to do. I think when we got married, it was no secret. You got married, and this was your husband. You know, it's not like that today. People get married, and after six months, they don't want to be married anymore. But when we got married, we knew that that was it. Not to say there weren't ups and downs, but we were married.

*Leon* We had our disputes but nothing radical. No earth-shaking problems. We've had the problems that I'm certain come with all marriages. However, back in that room, when you had me put my arm around Harriett, I still get a tingle. What do you want me to say? I still get a tingle! I like her! I love her! That's the words to describe it. When we were going out before we were married, I had some girlfriends in Philadelphia, but I could never get Harriett out of my mind. I always knew it was going to be Harriett.

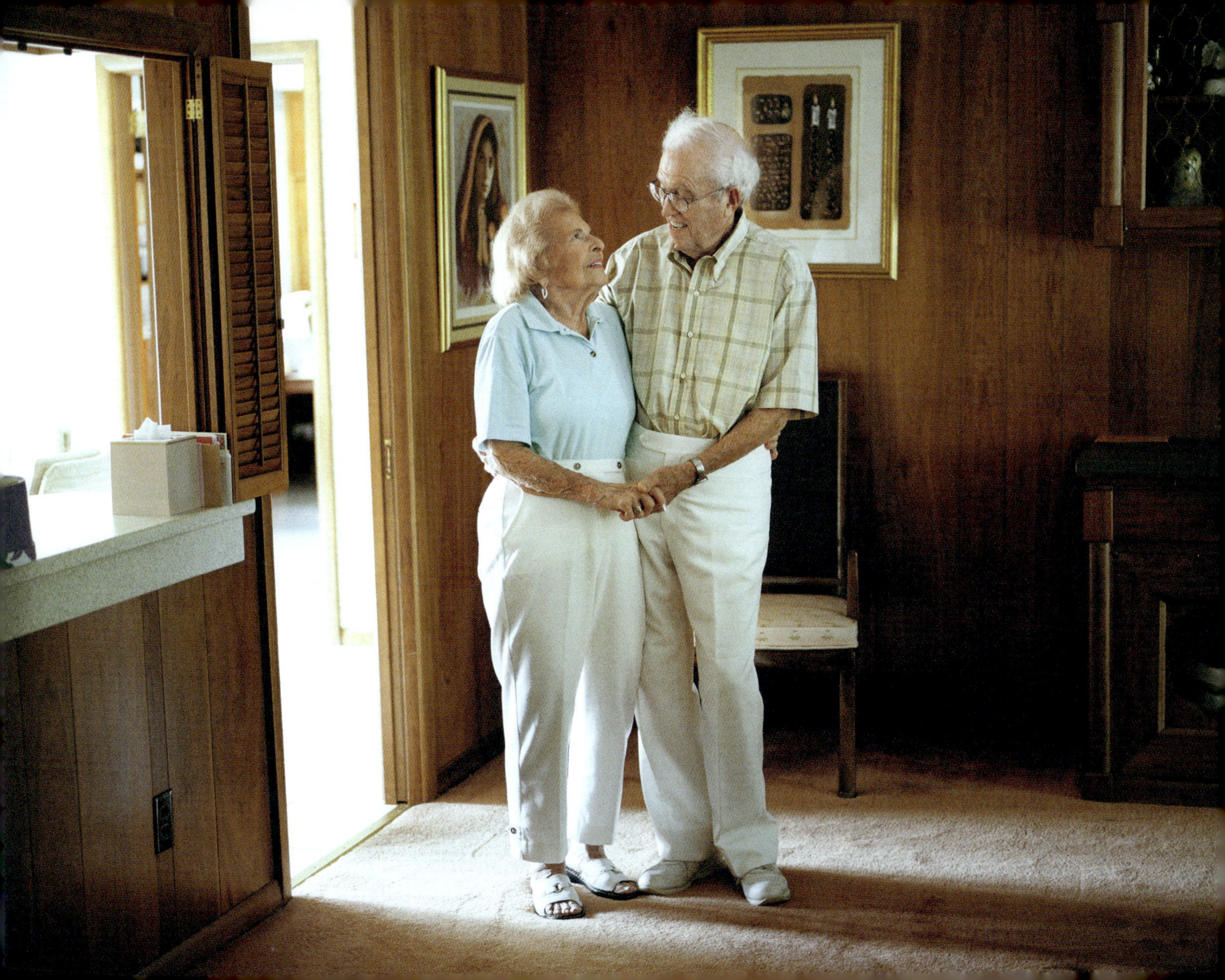

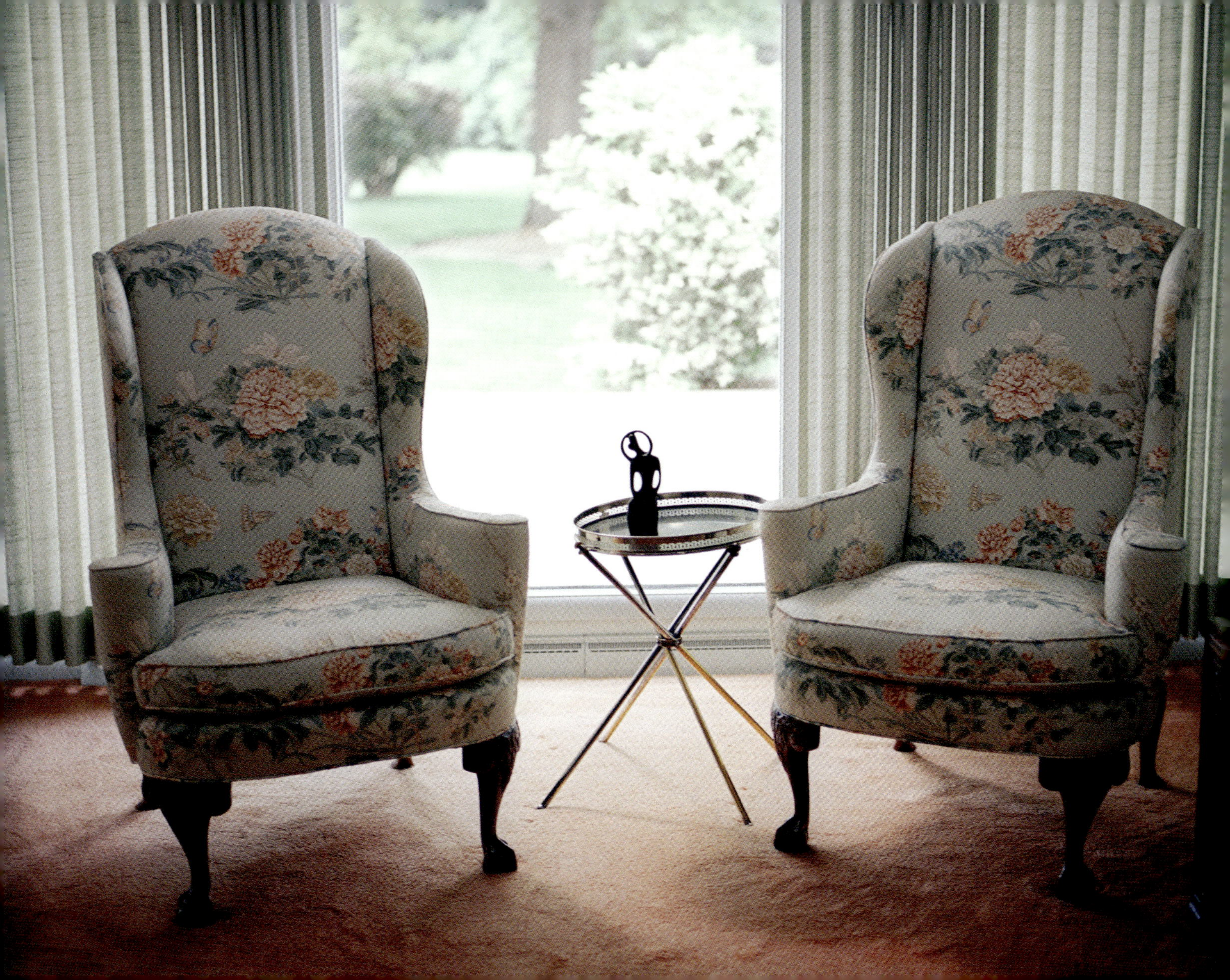

## Theauther and Annie Love

Brooklyn, New York

Married on December 23, 1950



*Theauther* I courted her a long time—a long, long time. I was in the navy for two years, and when I got out, I farmed. I farmed one year and I made a lot of money and I had bought a '56 Ford. And I was kinda wild at that time too. I used to come to her house and it was like a sandy row and I used to just swing around in her yard—just make circles out in her yard. And she'd come out and get in the car and we'd talk.

*Annie* In Georgia all of us used to stay at my old man's place, and Theauther used to come round. We lived at a saw mill and he used to come with his grandfather and they would get wood and be in the wagon. But the first time we really met was in 1944. At church we used to have sale boxes to raise money. But I never used to get much, maybe 50 cents or 75 cents. And they would say, "Do you want to bet higher? Who gives the next bid on the box?"

*Theauther* I knew that nobody was gonna buy it but me. I didn't care how much the bidding price was. I was going to buy it.

*Annie* So I think my box went up $1.50. That night he walked me home with my mother and my father. So from then on we'd see one another. Talk to each other.

*Theauther* We were young, and we didn't know what love was all about. But afterward we found out what love was. Love is sharing with one another. Don't care what you have, you share. And be willing to give. Another thing I tell people now is that you got to be able to bend a little bit. Because if the Lord hadn't made a tree that was kinda wavy, it would break. So that's love. Love is a powerful thing if you know what it means.

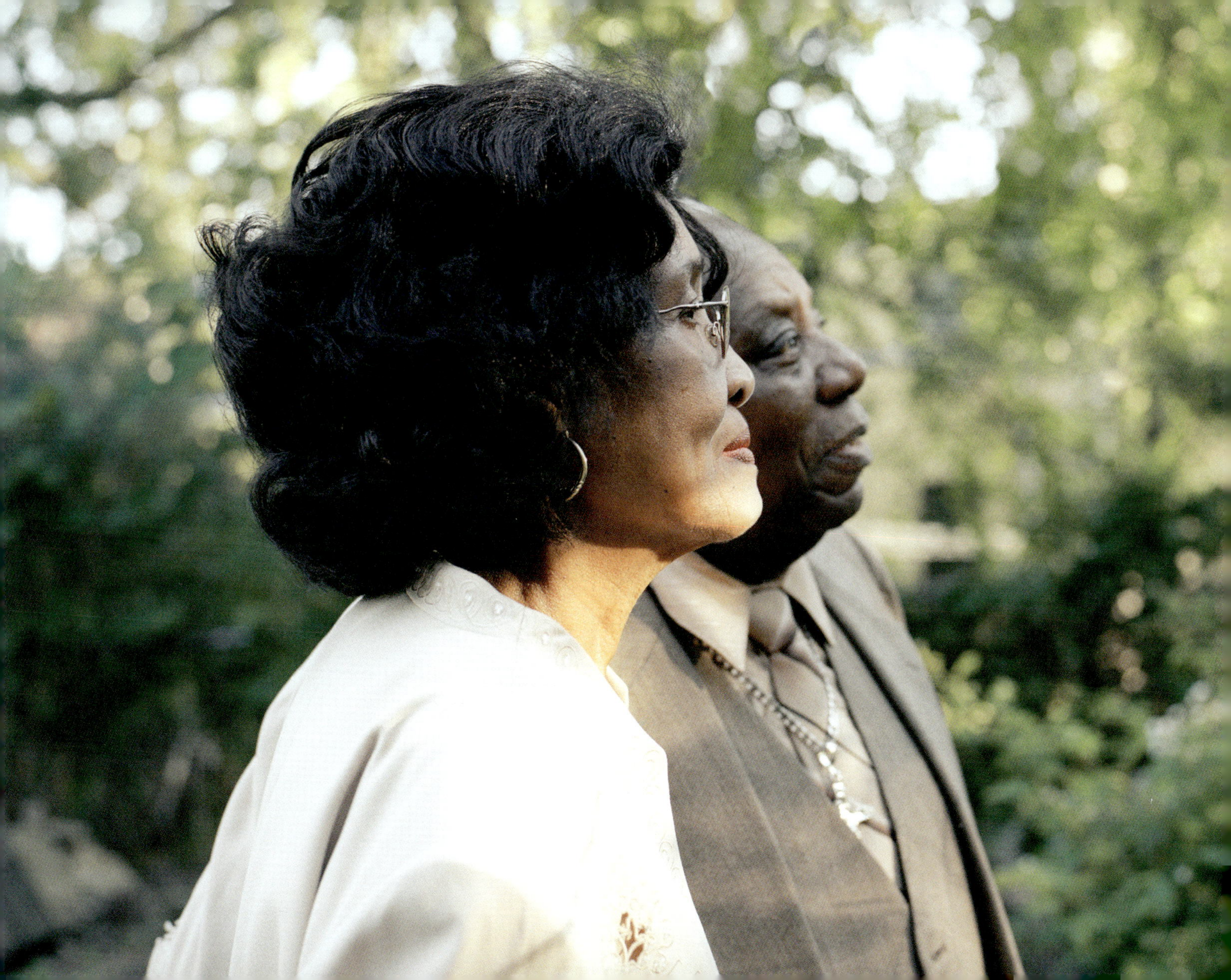

## Tom and Betty Fitzharris

Eastchester, New York

Married on January 16, 1943



*Betty* Now it's just the two of us in the house, just Tom and I. And I think we had good examples. His mother and father, my mother and father, both of them were married for years. Tom and I, we're aging together, we're doing it together. We both get sleepy at the same time. It's a completely different life than the one we had.

But I don't think he could get along without me to tell you the truth. More so now than ever before. I'm going to be 90 in June, and Tom is now 91. But, yes, we're getting to that age, you know. And I think we're so blessed to be in this house alone. I spoil him because I do everything. The wash, the cooking, the shopping. I don't expect much. He was never really much one to do the cooking or anything like that. So he says I spoil him. I think he does appreciate me in a different way now that we're older.

*Tom* Betty and I were compatible without working at it. For some reason or other we just got along real well. It wasn't a case of I had to do this or she had to do that.

To me, it's a difficult thing to say how it is that we've been married for so long and we're still talking to each other and we're still compatible. Whether you've seen it or not, we've seen people, been with people that have been married awhile, but there seems to be a little friction. And we've had our differences, too, that's for sure.

Love has helped me live as long as I have. It's made me realize how lucky I am. I've said this to my daughter—the best thing that happened to me in my lifetime was marrying Betty. I've been very lucky in that way. I was educated, I was in the marines, I went to Notre Dame. We've got three good children. We have six grandchildren. I really can't ask for anything more. We count our blessings, believe me. We've been blessed.

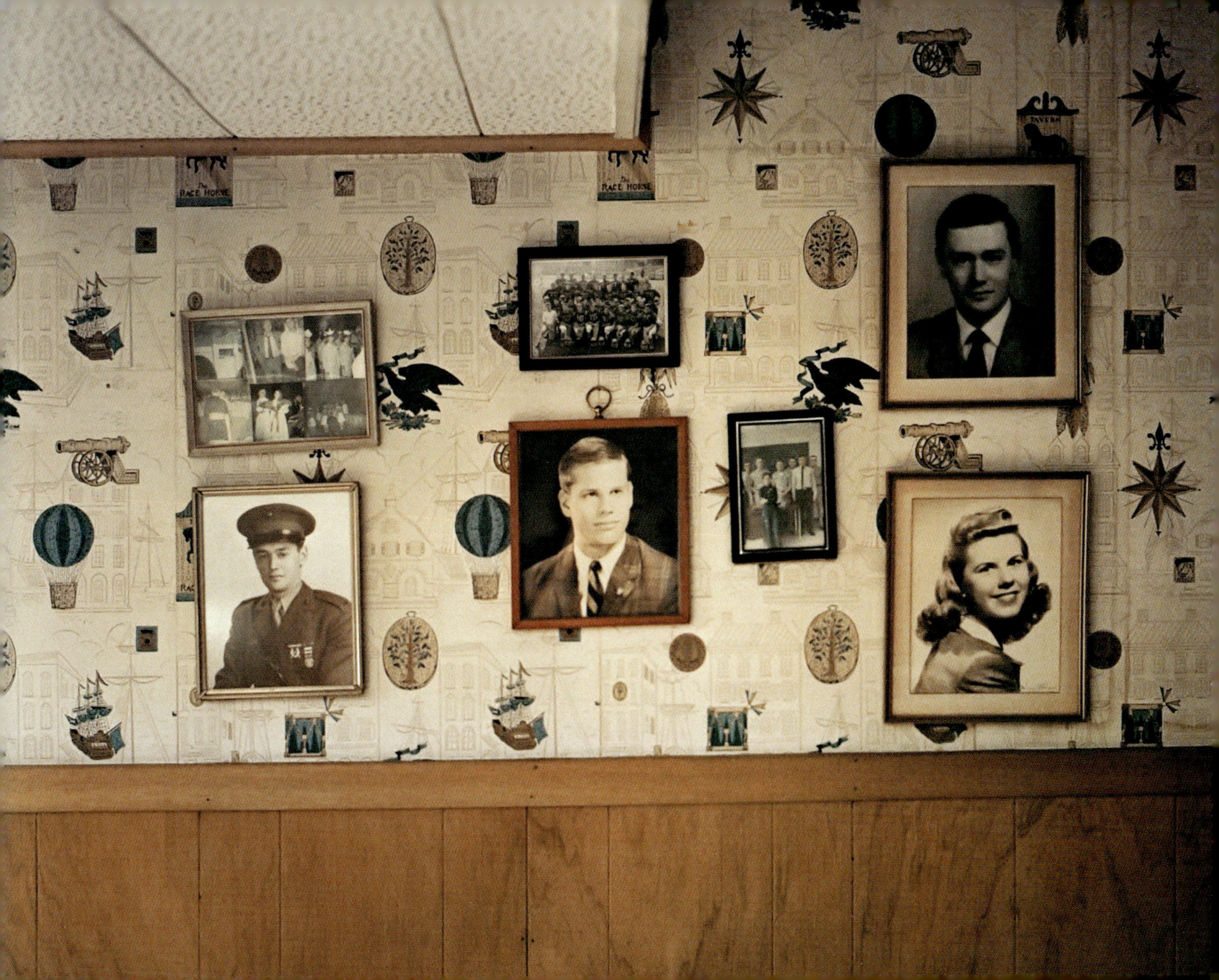
The RACE HORSE
The RACE HORSE

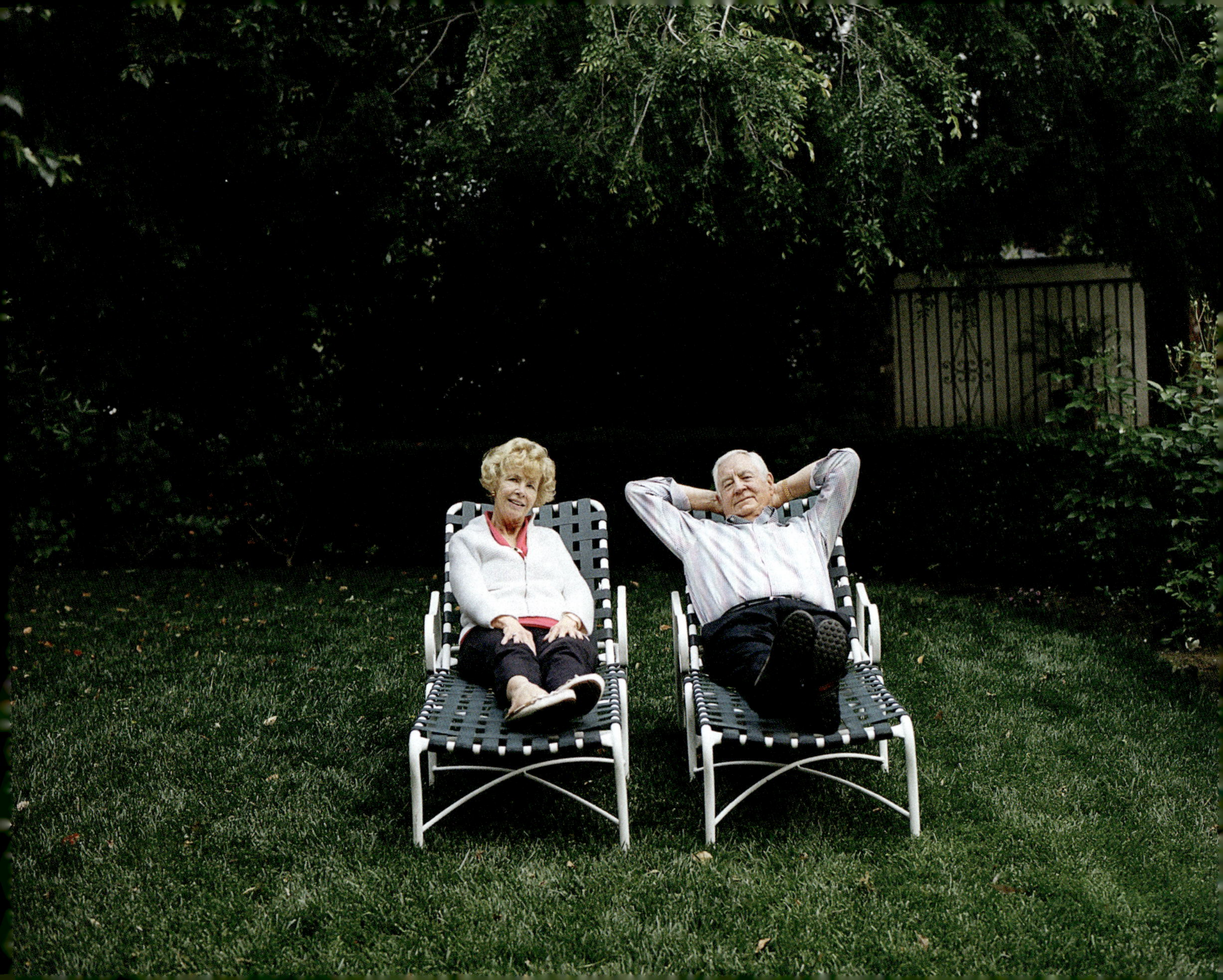

## Richard and Julianne Gunter

La Canada, California

Married on September 11, 1961



*Dick* We've had a lot of fortunate things happen in our marriage that have worked out really well for us. The first one being when I asked her out. We dated all during high school, and a lot of kids got married early in those years. We all knew we were going to grow up and get married and have 2.3 children and 2.3 cars, that's the way we grew up. But I was absolutely scared to death to get married. I mean, in the course of 50 years, Julie can finish my sentences, and I can finish her sentences, but I suspect I was probably extremely insecure at the thought of providing for a family.

When we were in college, I brought her home from a date one night and walked her to the door, and she said, "I never want to see you again." Just like that, you know, this was out of the blue. In retrospect we probably were fighting that night, but you know, this was not exactly what I expected. So I didn't call the next day, but a week later I bought some roses and had them sent over to her house with a note. And what I didn't know was that Julie had left on vacation with the family for a week so when she came back, there were some dead roses on her front porch, and she said, "Well, now, this is really appropriate." So we didn't see each other for two years.

I was thinking about her all the time but too proud to do anything about it, and subsequently I find out that she was also thinking about me. I heard Julie was engaged to be married, and I thought this is too small a community, we're going to run into each other, and I absolutely cannot run into Julie after she's married. I would be lost, and I wouldn't know what to say. So I called her up at the sorority house, and she came on and I said, "Hi, this is Dick Gunter." And she said, "I know who this is." I asked her if she would like to get a cup of coffee, and she said, "Yes." I picked her up, and Julie told me that she was never really going to marry this person. She just offered that. And by the time we finished, we just knew we were going to get married.

I was lucky to make a good enough living early on that allowed Julie to stay home, and Julie did save money for the family by being at home. She was frugal, she was smart, she took care of things and she didn't waste anything. So I think both of us literally felt whatever we have was both ours. It's not mine and it's not yours, it's what we did together.

I was in the brokerage business, and as a trader you rely on and use other traders and share information. It's difficult to justify to someone who doesn't understand, but it's the old three-martini lunch. A bunch of guys are getting together and having lunch and drinks and talking about what they did today and this stock and that stock and what's going up and what's going down. So it was enjoyable, but there actually was a business purpose behind it. In hindsight, was I selfish with Julie in not telling her I'm going to be late? You just go out, and if it's three o'clock, four o'clock, five o'clock, six o'clock, you know, you just justify it in that you're doing business. When you're a young man and things are going your way, you tend to think that you deserve everything you have. Maybe you just get a little full of yourself with success. And I came home late one day and I come walking in the kitchen in my good suit and good tie and say hi and she's feeding our eldest son in the kitchen with some Gerber baby food and I walked in with my hi. She took the spoon, dipped it in the carrots, held it up with her finger and threw the carrots without saying a word. Right all over from my chin all down my tie. I ended up laughing and Julie ended up laughing, but she did get her point across.

Being in love is wonderful, but you have to work at staying in love. Our daughter used to kid us because she said, "Boy, all my high school friends just think it's great the way you hug Mom or you'll kiss Mom when you come home." So maybe we did that a little more than some people. I think that physical communication by touching somebody is profound compared to just saying hello or hi. We both try to think of what the other person is thinking. We both try to see the other person's point of view. After this many years, Julie knows how I am going to react, and I know how she's going to react. I like a movie with a lot of people getting shot, and Julie likes a movie with love and romance. So we watch one of mine, and we watch one of hers.

You have to respect the other person. I mean, I am so fortunate. I don't want to embarrass Julie, but literally everybody thinks she's the sweetest person in the world. Julie's the kind that she can't do enough for you. In my business with traders, it's a high testosterone business, and I knew an awful lot of guys that did what they wanted to do. They were good guys, but their family didn't come first, and I don't think their wife came first. And now I see in the last 10 years or so, I see these guys turning 65 and I see them retiring and all of a sudden, they get up in the morning and they ask their wives what are they going to do that day. And if the wife goes to the store, they want to go to the store with them. And so my point is be aware of age and what it does to you. Some of your value systems change, some of the independence isn't quite the thing that it was when you were 30. When you're 65 or 70, trust me, you're going to want to know what your wife is doing and why she's not inviting you to go with her. And it can almost be a reversal of roles.

## Albert "Kay" McKay and Delsa Erickson

Star Valley, Wyoming
Married on April 9, 1951



*Kay* We've always lived right here in Star Valley, and I tell people we never had enough money to get out! That's the reason we stayed. But we wouldn't leave if we could. We have seven children and 27 grandchildren. Delsa, she's always been a home wife. And so if we've had success in our family, I attribute it to the fact that she stayed home with the children and took care of them. I'd say if we were going to be paid for the way we raised our kids, she would get 75 percent.

*Delsa* And we've done a lot of things together. I even helped drive a gas truck when Kay had the Chevron station. Not the big long ones but one with 2000 gallons.

*Kay* We'd go on to the farmers and deliver the fuel to them so that they could do their farming. This used to be a pretty good place for loggers, but with the environmentalists and whatnot, they just about shut that off. But we used to go out into the mountains with our delivery truck. We would drive together up to the junction, and I would go one way with a load of fuel for an oil rig and she would go into Jackson Hole with a load of gas for the station there. One time we were taking a load of fuel to a logging company back in the mountains, and we got back in there OK, but it started to snow and kept up for hours and hours and we got marooned in there. They had to come in on snow wheels and liberate us. That helped us come together, too.

*Delsa* I remember getting on the CB and saying, "Kay, don't you dare eat that last sandwich!"

They say that a successful marriage is a 50/50. You give and take. And I believe it's probably more on the giving part than 50 percent. You have to pretty well give yourself, taking into consideration your partner's wants and likes and dislikes and what would be best for the two of you. Our religion helps our marriage and makes it strong. You don't just walk away when things don't go just like you want them to. I think the promise that we've made to one another is so important that we wouldn't just walk away.

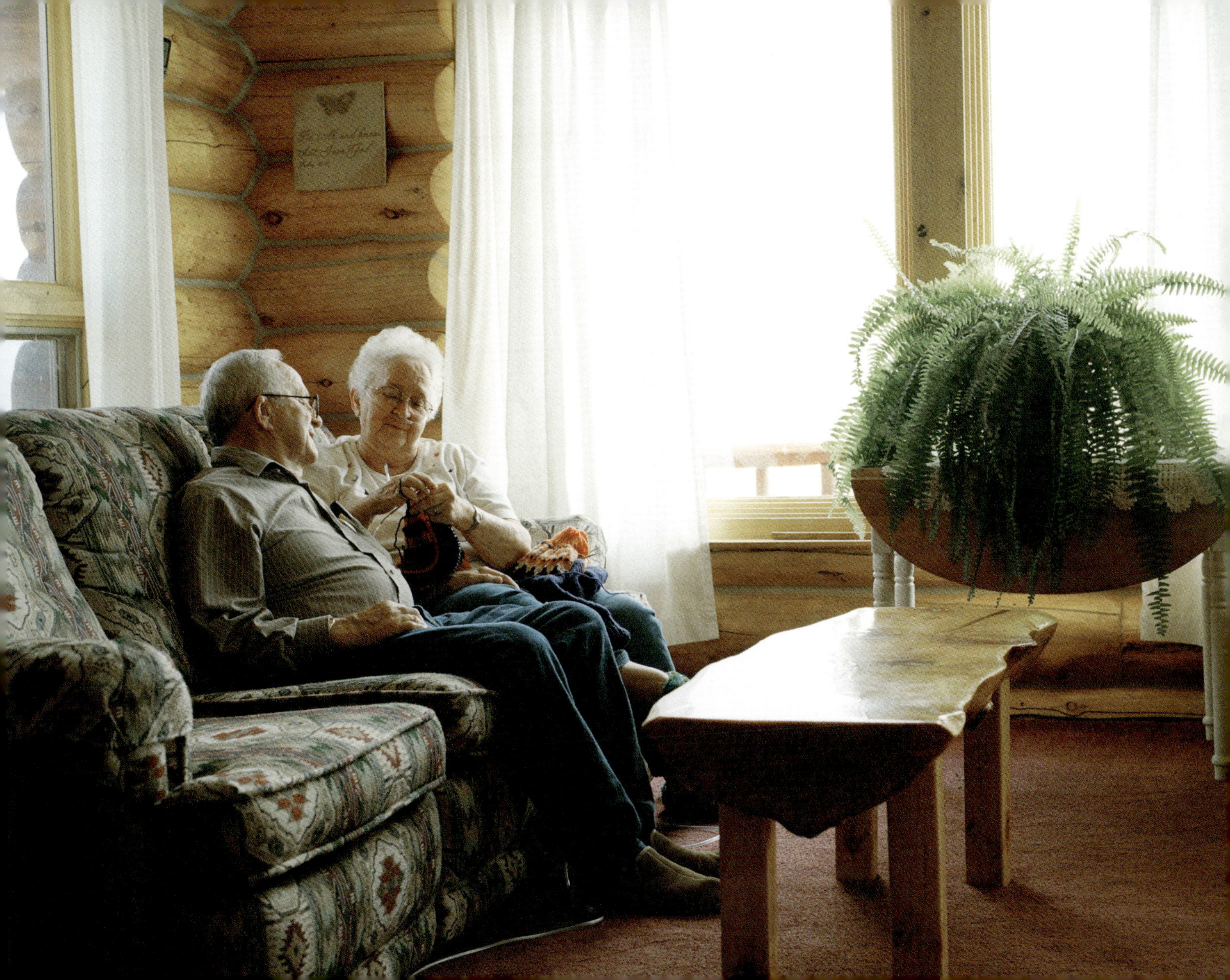

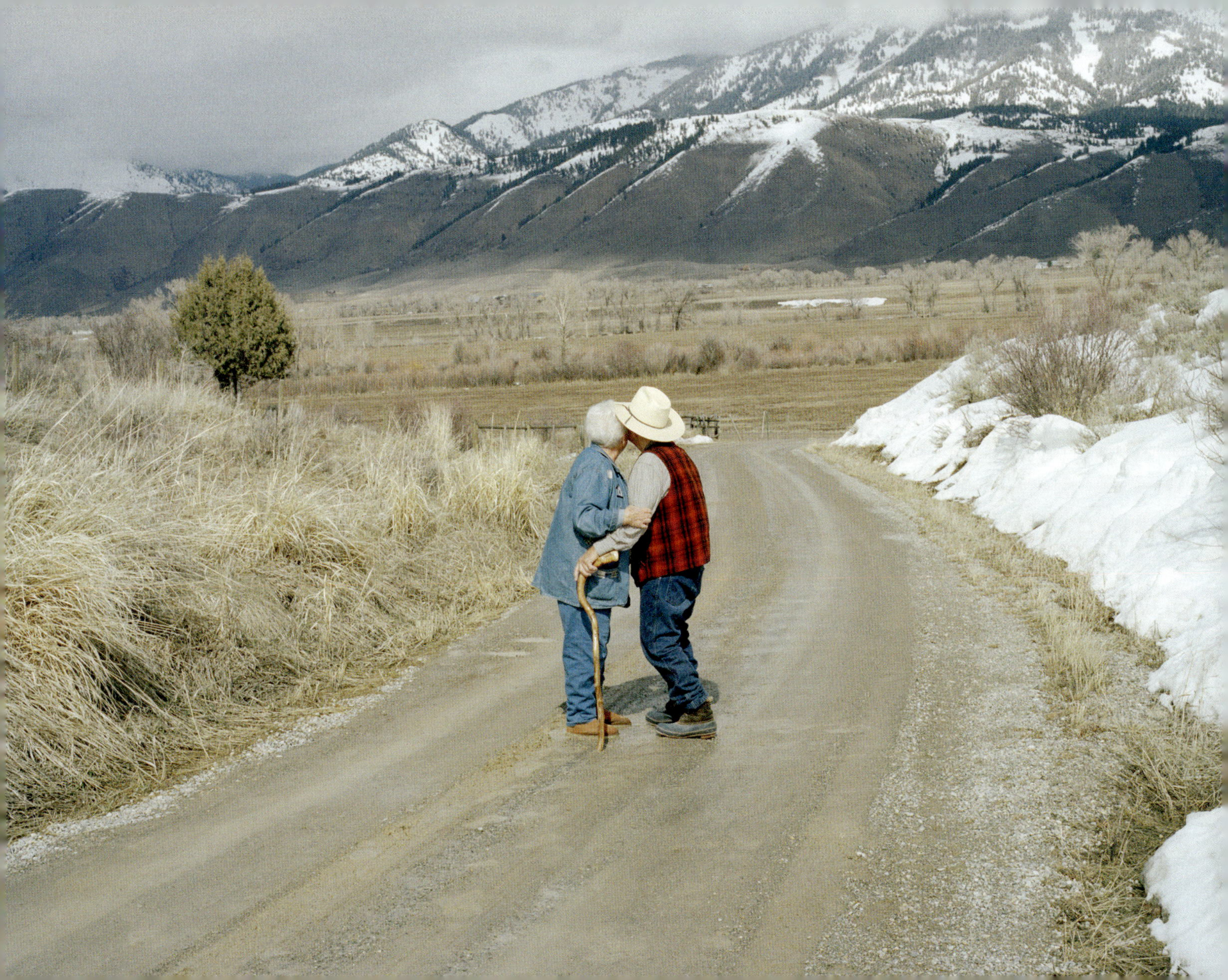

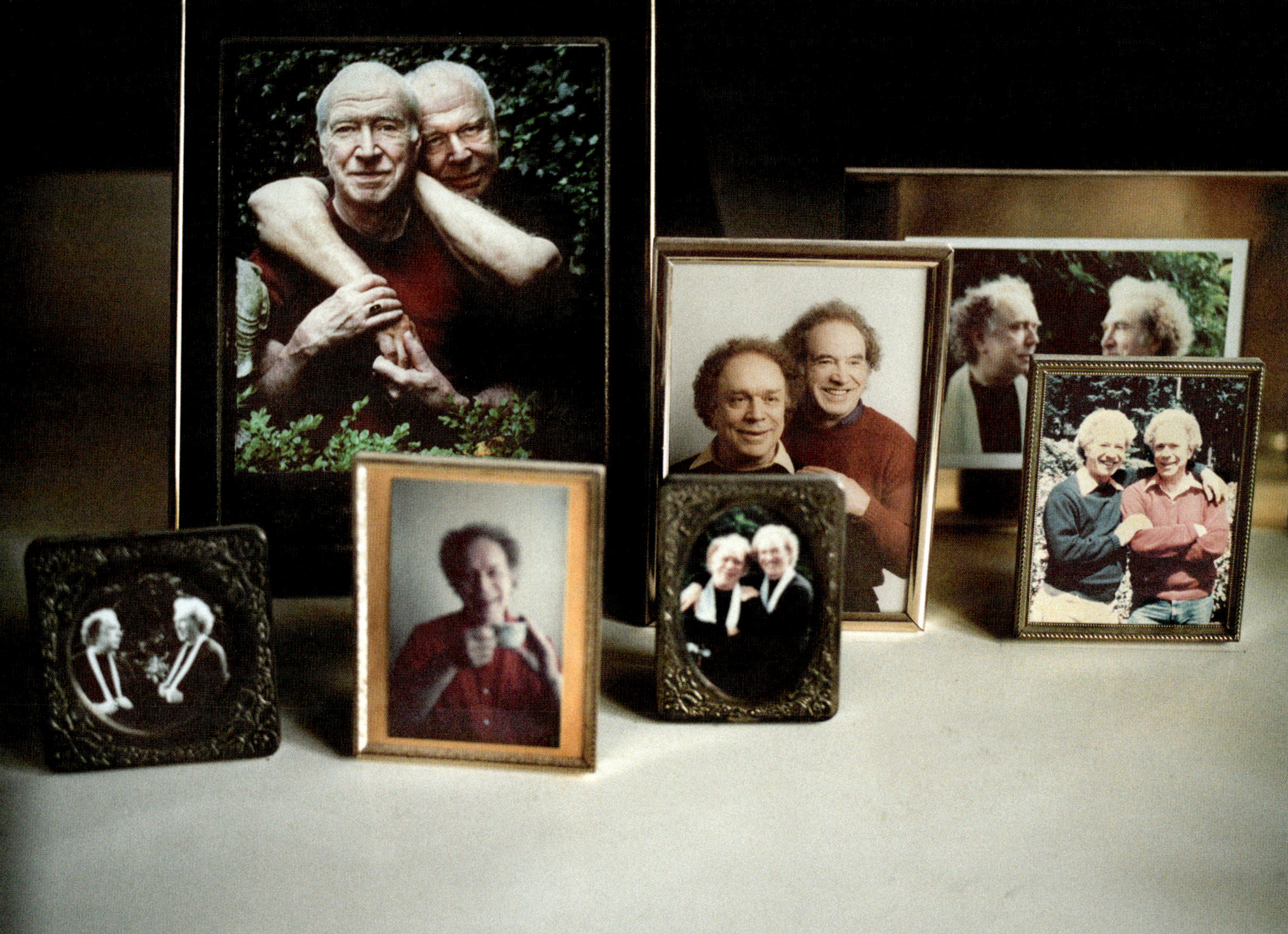

## Eric Marcoux and Eugene Woodworth

Portland, Oregon

Together since June 13, 1953

*Eric* It will be 60 years in June, and on our first date, the waitress said, "Oh, are you twins?" In old photographs it's hard to discern who's who until we look really closely. We both looked young, and we were both conventionally attractive. At any rate the waitress asked us that, and it was intuitive on our part to say, "Yes." And so we lived formally as brothers for at least a couple of decades. There is still a share of people who ask if we are related. It used to be safer to say that we were brothers. You've given me the opportunity to say, "No, I'm not his brother. I'm his lover or his husband." Whatever you can listen to at the moment and that I love him. Thank you for giving me a chance to tell someone that I really do love him and very deeply.

*Eugene* Love is something you feel way before you know it's happening. On the day we met, I was having lunch with a friend of mine after having been to the lakes with him in Chicago. We were sitting across from each other and after a while something appeared behind my shoulder and my body went cold and electricity ran through it and I thought,



"Oh Lord, what's happening?" I couldn't move. And the conversation between the two of them was, "Oh, hi Eric. I'm having a party this evening. Would you like to come?" And Eric said, "Thank you, Nathan. No, I'm going to the movies with some friends, but thank you anyway." And he disappeared.

And I could finally breathe, and I thought, "Oh, thank God that's over—whatever that was." And all of a sudden, the same thing appeared again—the same reaction. And I couldn't see. I couldn't turn my head. And he came over. He said, "Nathan, since I'm coming to your party tonight, don't you think you should introduce me to your friend?" So we got introduced, and I turned and shook hands with him and that was the beginning.

*Eric* On my part, I was very depressed. I was going with my friends to see a movie, and in those days I was a very, very shy unassertive sort of person. So when I encounter my friend Nathan with a strange person sitting to his side at whom I almost didn't look at all, it was about all I could do to be assertive enough to say, "No, I'm going to a movie with other people." And I went and sat down. And it's like a paranormal experience on some level. What I felt was something put its fingers, arms, hands under my armpits and lifted me and marched me back to the side of the table. And I found myself again being more than forward by my standards then because I said, "Nathan, I've changed my mind. I am going to come to your party. And I think you should introduce me to your friend."

We went to the party, sometime went by, we made love and then for the next several months, we courted. And whereas I would have tried to skip that sequence, it's a sequence most of us understand. Our connections are likely, no matter how deeply they lead to love, they are likely to start out on a very biological level. So that's our story. I suppose it's another version of looking across the room and falling in love with someone. But what's really amazed me as I've moved into our 60th year is how many, many, many times I've fallen in love with him over and over again.

*Eugene* We say I love you at least a half a dozen times during the day.

*Eric* We do and we say that to one another over the past several years. I remember—I remind myself of those moments that are quite frequent of what he says and how he touches me and how I touch him in return. There are the deserts we move through. The dull, boring things we move through. We move through with jobs. We get over the honeymoon with the job. We get over the honeymoon with a new piece of furniture. You get over a honeymoon as a monk or a nun with a relationship with God. And then there are long, dry periods and to know that, well that's just the nature of intimacy.

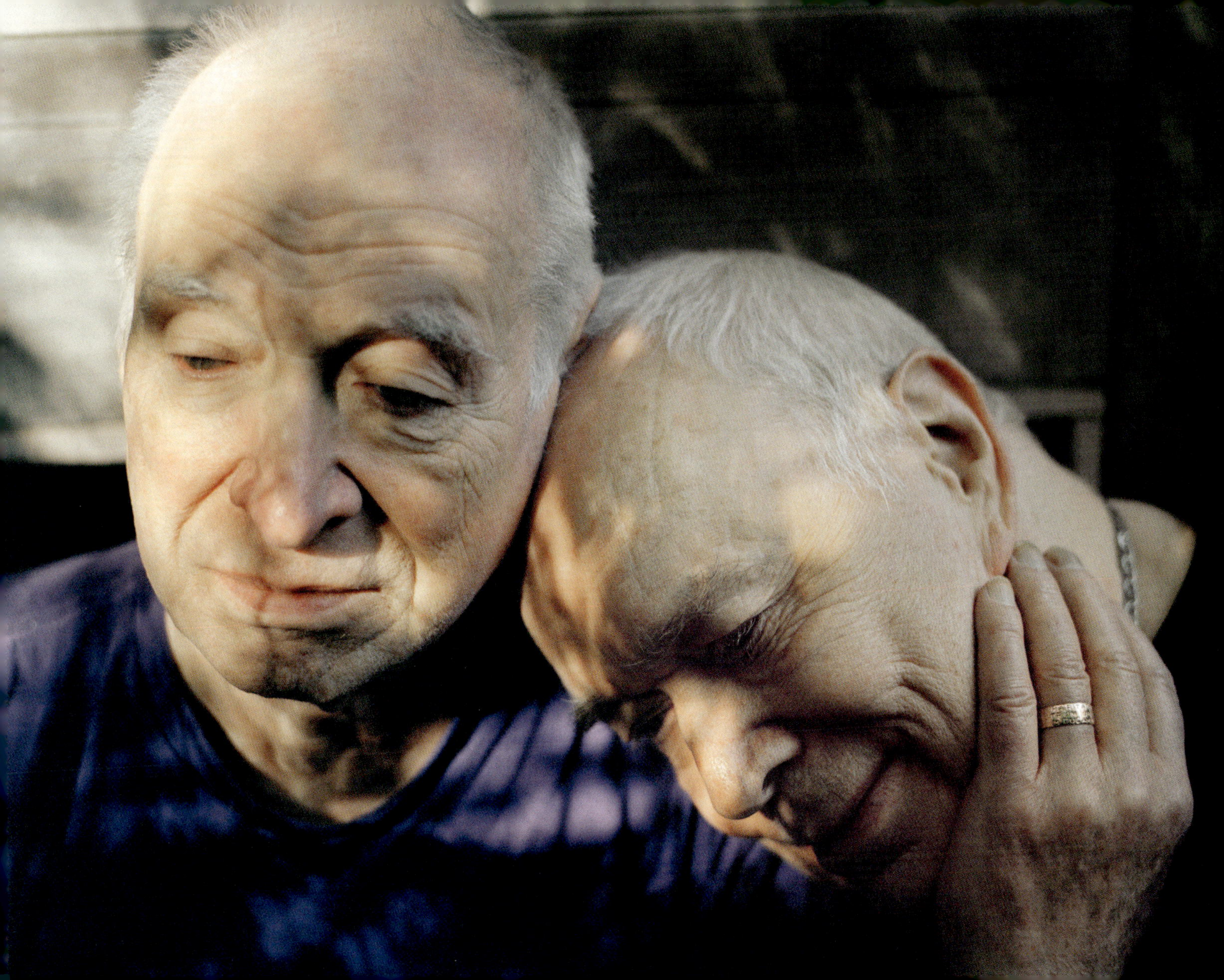

## John and Sherma Campbell

Star Valley, Wyoming
Married on May 13, 1955



*Sherma* When I was 13 years old, I was walking up the street with my girlfriend, and we had just moved to Afton, Wyoming. As we approached, we met John and his friend Ray, and we stood and talked to them for a while like most teenagers do. After they went on their way, we giggled a little bit, and I said, "I'm gonna marry John Campbell!" And she said, "You can't. He's my boyfriend!" And I said, "Well, OK, but someday I'm going to marry him!" And, of course, we were really too young to date, but that's the first time I'd met him and that's when I picked him out.

When I turned 17, I wanted to get married, and my parents were really disgruntled about that. They wanted so much for me to finish high school, which I hadn't. I did later. We got married in the Salt Lake Latter-day Saints Temple. And we mostly did that to satisfy my parents. It made them feel better because we believe when we're married there, we're married forever and ever. For all eternity, even after we die, we have our families sealed to us forever. I think when hard times came in our marriage that was something that kind of glued us together because we had that belief. There was no divorce, not that I haven't thought about it. But, no, it made us work harder.

We're pretty much as different as black and white. He was a very laid-back, happy-go-lucky cowboy. I came from a family of English people that were taught very proper manners. I liked the finer things of life. So we had to compromise a lot, and love carried us through. I used to go riding with him up in the hills and camping on the ground in little makeshift tents and sometimes no tents. And then he would go to the concert with me. We tried to enjoy it for one another. I was always quite a shy girl, and John was extroverted. And so when we would mingle in social situations, I would pretty much hide behind him and let him take care of it. And it always worked.

I have to admit, I was drawn to John. Why I chose him the first time I met him I don't know. Something spoke to me, I think, just as a very young teenager. As time has gone on, I've learned to love him even more. Being around him made me feel like more of a person. When you start out, you think you love each other as much as you possibly can, but love grows—just like your inner self grows as time goes by and you have experiences. And now at this stage of the game, I love him even more. I can't even imagine life without him.

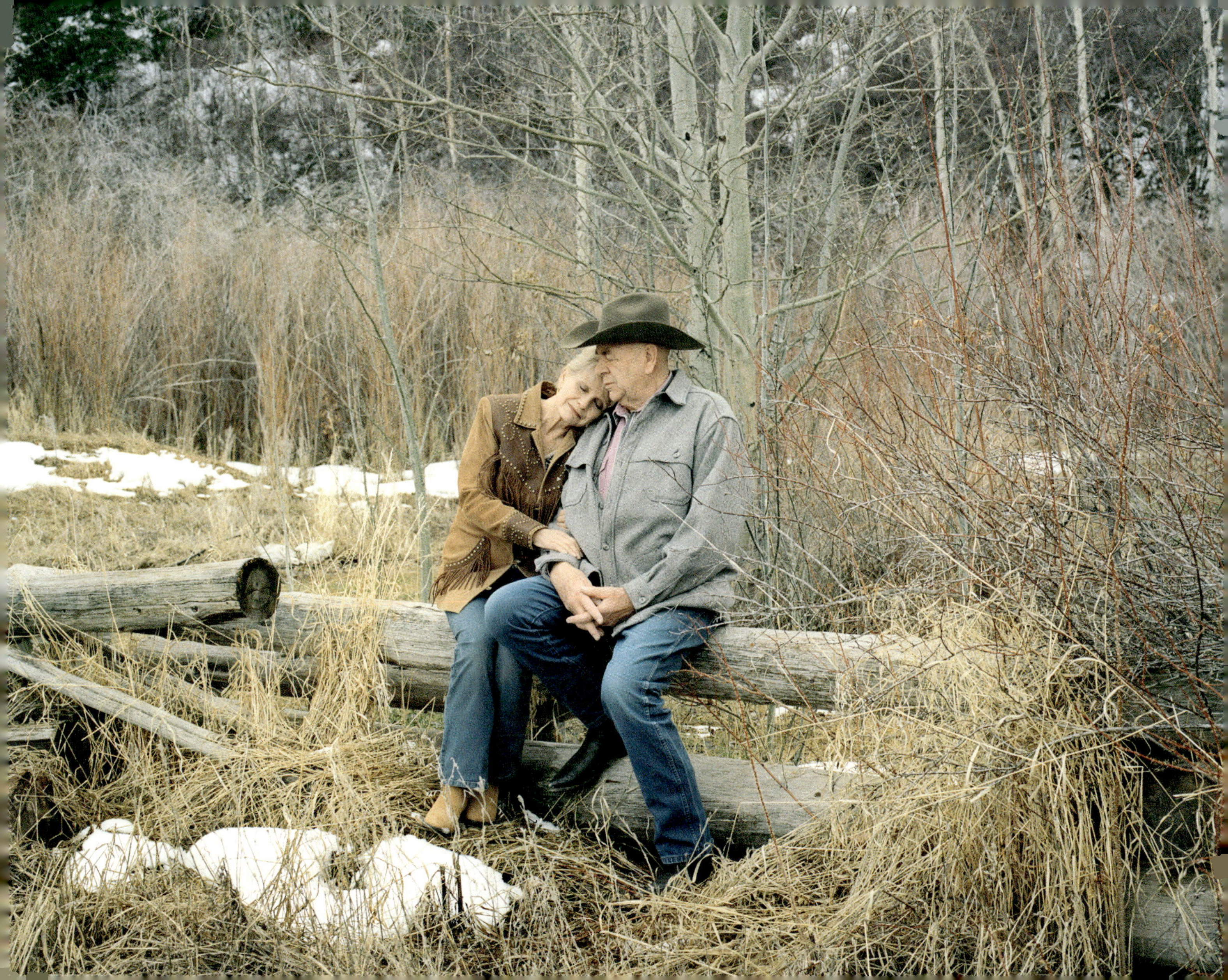

## David and Sheila Newman

Brooklyn, New York
Married on April 12, 1957



*Sheila* It was my mother who had suggested that I go see David because I had to write a music paper, and I had never written anything about music. So I went over, and I thought maybe he would write it for me. But he said, "No, I'll help you, but you have to write it yourself." He always had very high standards, much higher than mine. In everything. So after we wrote the paper together, he suddenly says, "I'm going to a party with some of the guys from the army." So he took me out that night, and he was very friendly. And you know, I had never thought of him romantically. But he looked at me like a man who was just coming out of the army would look at a sexy woman.

Of course my parents were thrilled because in those days if you were graduating college and you didn't have a ring on your finger, you were going to be an old maid. And I had two sisters and a grandmother, and my father was surrounded by all these women. He couldn't wait for me to move out. The oldest daughter! "He's wonderful, you should marry him!" Right from the beginning. So in three months I think he barely asked me to marry him, my mother already called up the wedding hall. David was a little shocked.

In my house my father had handled all the bills, but my mother was handy around the house. I never learned that from her, I can't do a thing, and that was a big problem when we first got married. I remember when somebody came and the house was a mess, I'd say, "I'm sorry about this house but my husband's a terrible housekeeper." I'd say that, and they were shocked because everyone was so conventional. Everybody thought that a woman has to run the house.

David always supported any interests I had. He supported me with whatever I did, told me I should do the best I can. And I was anti-intellectual when I married him. I got to love music because he practiced a lot and I listened to him and he explained everything. We really changed, we enriched each other's lives.

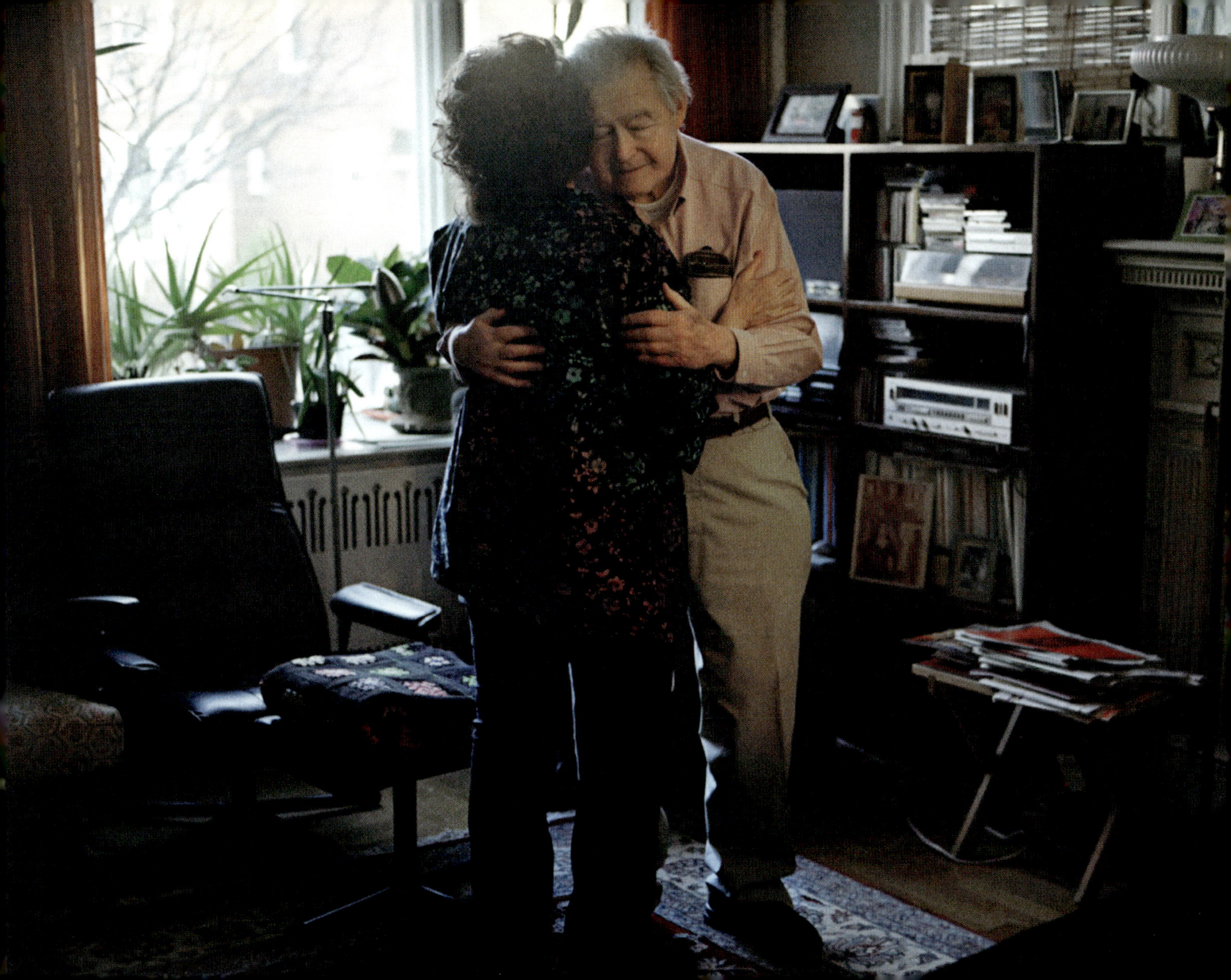

## Jin Lin and Lai Mei Chen

Brooklyn, New York
Married on February 4, 1961



*Jin Lin* We lived very far apart, and at that time we didn't even have a telephone. So when I returned home, we sent letters. We wrote letters each week, but it took about 20 days for our letters to reach each other. We did this for five years.

We had so many things in common it was like our hearts were the same. I love that we get along and that we can talk all the time. Even though I grew up in Shanghai, I worked and studied in Guangzhou. To see each other, the train tickets were very expensive. It was around 70 dollars from Guangzhou to Tianjin. Fortunately, we didn't have too many responsibilities to our families, and we were able to save money for the ticket to see each other. We'd work to make money for the train tickets that would take us to each other.

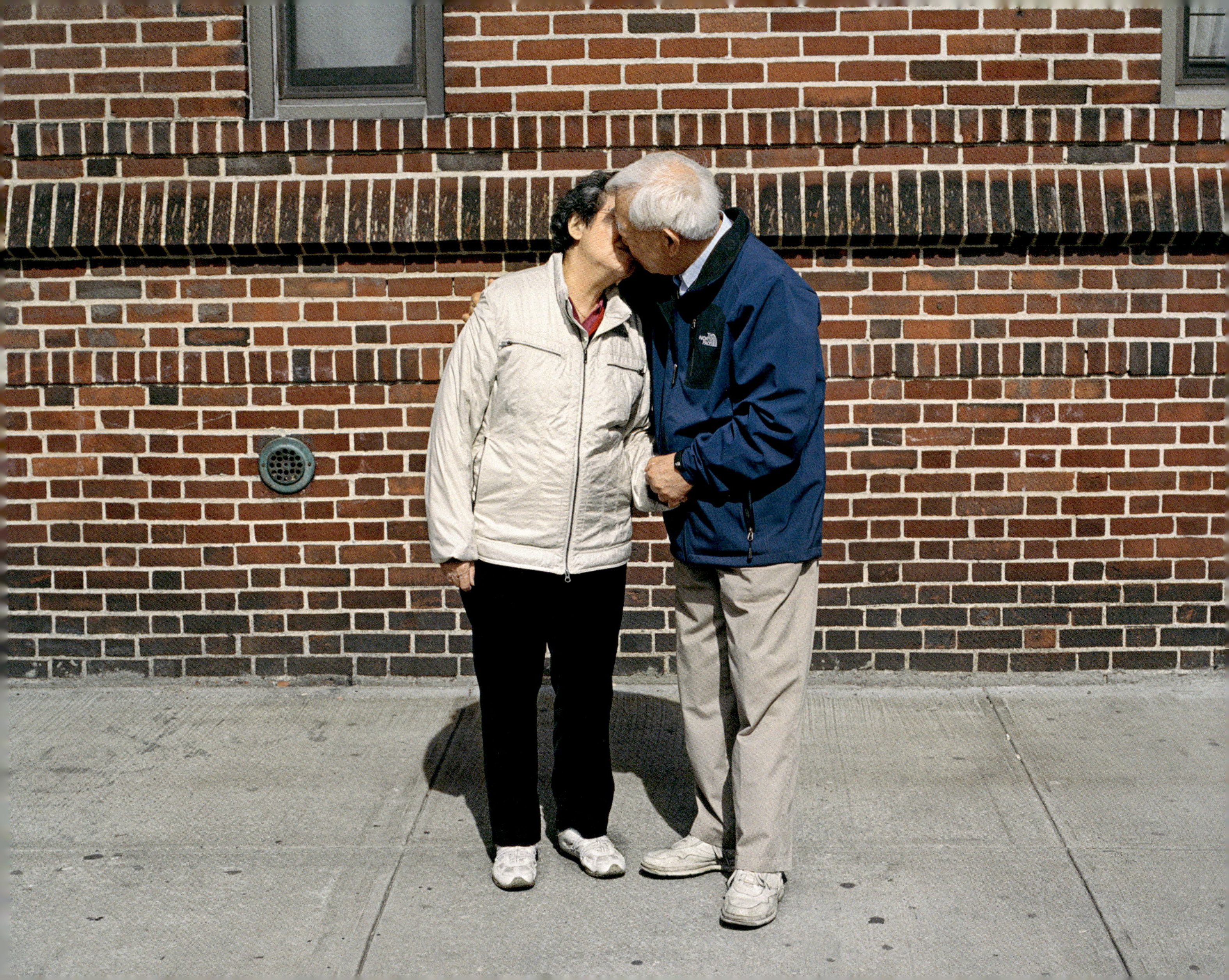

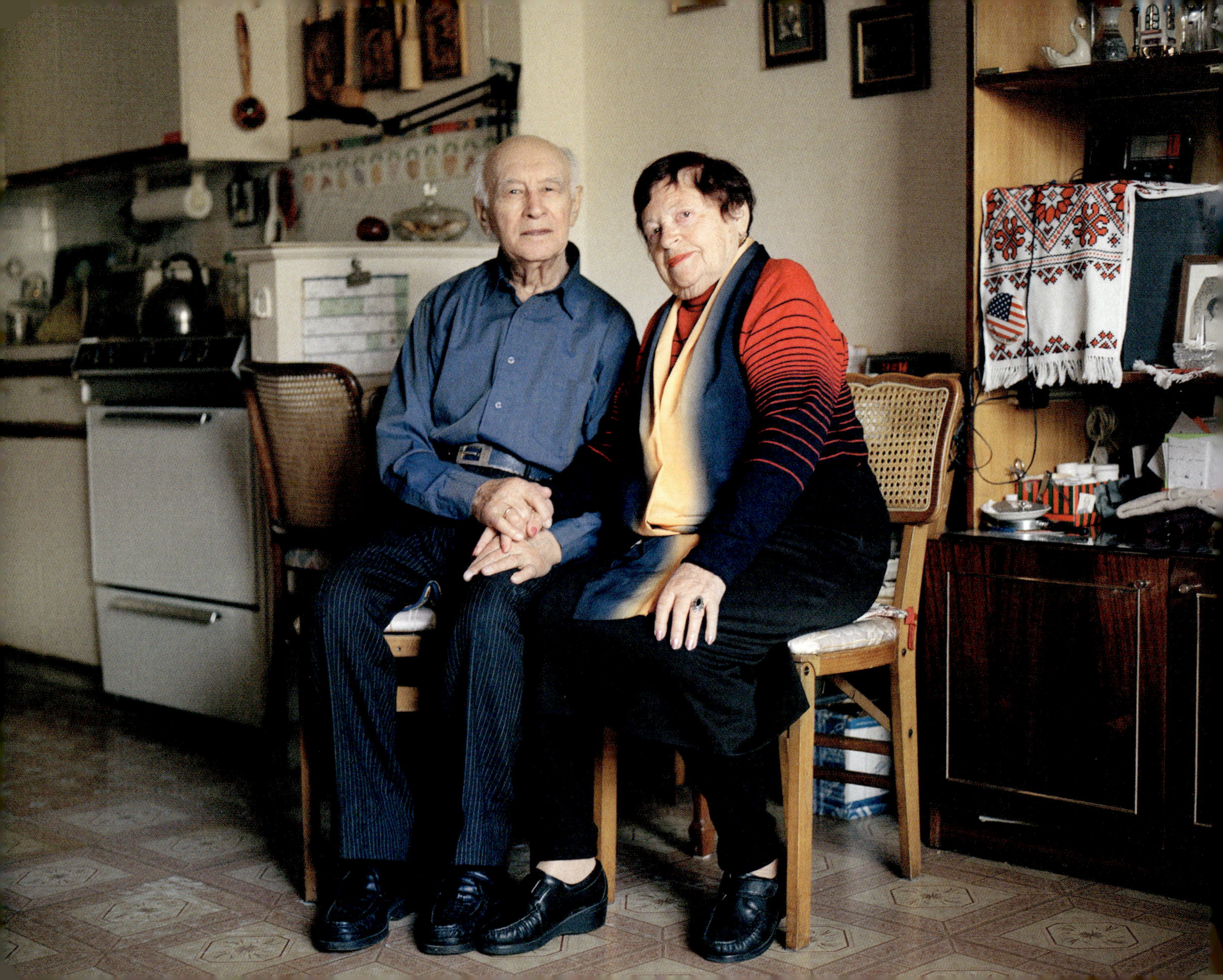

## Mikhail and Evgenia Gurevich

Brooklyn, New York

Married on March 6, 1946

*Evgenia* We were married in March of 1946, not so long ago. I remember this day like it was yesterday. He came from the army. He was wounded. He was sick. But with great pleasure, I accepted him at the hospital in Czechoslovakia. From this time we were both together.

We came to America and America helped him. He had a lot of treatments, and this is why he is alive. I knew him since he was a child. And for me, he is a child now too! I didn't forget. For me, he is number one, and I try to have him as long as I can.

*Mikhail* And about you?

*Evgenia* What about me? Nothing about me. About you, this is the chips! Nothing about me.

OK, I was in the army too. Yes, I was. He was a soldier and I was a medical captain. We went to the front and took the wounded people. It was very, very hard. During the war my husband was shot. He didn't have anything to eat. He was very thin and very sick. Now he's perfect because America helped us. And we helped each other to survive.



I will tell you how we have been married this long. We love each other, we help each other and we try to do the best. Him for me and I for him. He does more than I do. Yes, I say he's better! He's quiet but that's what is necessary for a woman.

## James and Sandra Lambert Besser

Largo, Florida

Married on December 4, 1960



*Sandra* Even today, after almost 54 years, we go into a restaurant and look around and see all these people who have been together a long time, and they have nothing to say to one another. And we're chatting away like we just met. I don't think marriage is ever wonderful in the beginning of the relationship because you are two different people—sometimes two different backgrounds and there's a great deal of adjusting to do. And in today's world, sad to say, I see so many young people give up. And I mean, if that were the case, we would have given up many times. But you have to look at the total picture and work as a team and not always put yourself first. I don't mean losing your identity, but think of the other person. And in turn that other person thinks of you, and that makes a whole picture. I think a tribute to my husband is that he never tried to tell me how to do or live my life. I'm an independent person and he's secure as a male and that's never interfered with his thinking. I see other husbands who are so insecure in their own masculinity that they try to interfere with the growth of their wife. And this is what causes a lot of trouble. And that has never been an issue in my marriage. He's never stopped me for anything that I've wanted to do.

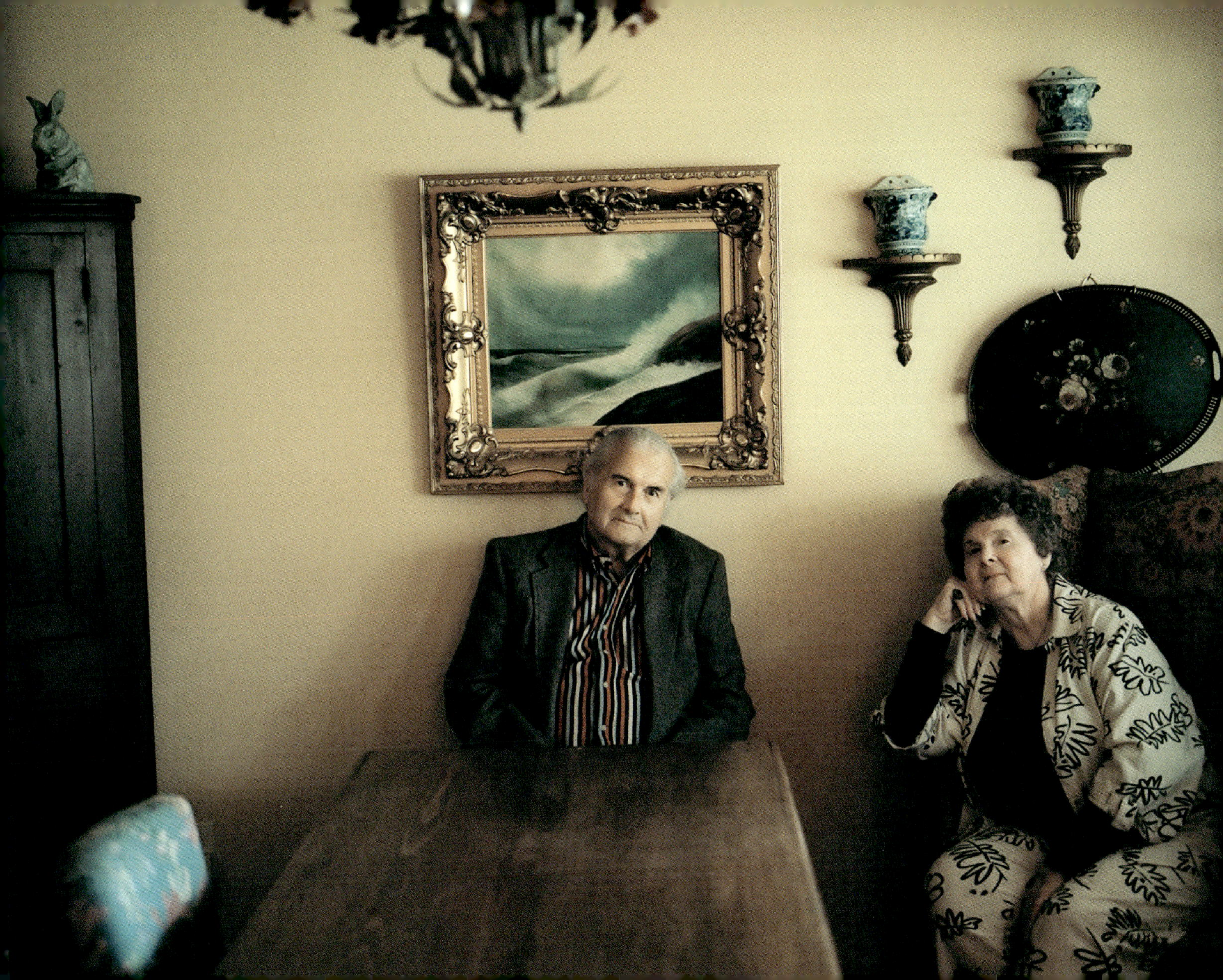

## Yevgeniy and Lyubov Kissin

Brooklyn, New York
Married on June 29, 1941



*Yevgeniy* We met at a dancing party. It was in January 1938. My friend invited me to the party, he said there would be a lot of beautiful young girls. Another cadet with high boots had approached her, but she didn't like high boots and so she said no to him. I was the second one to approach her. I had a different uniform, but I'm still not sure if it was my uniform or my face that attracted her to me.

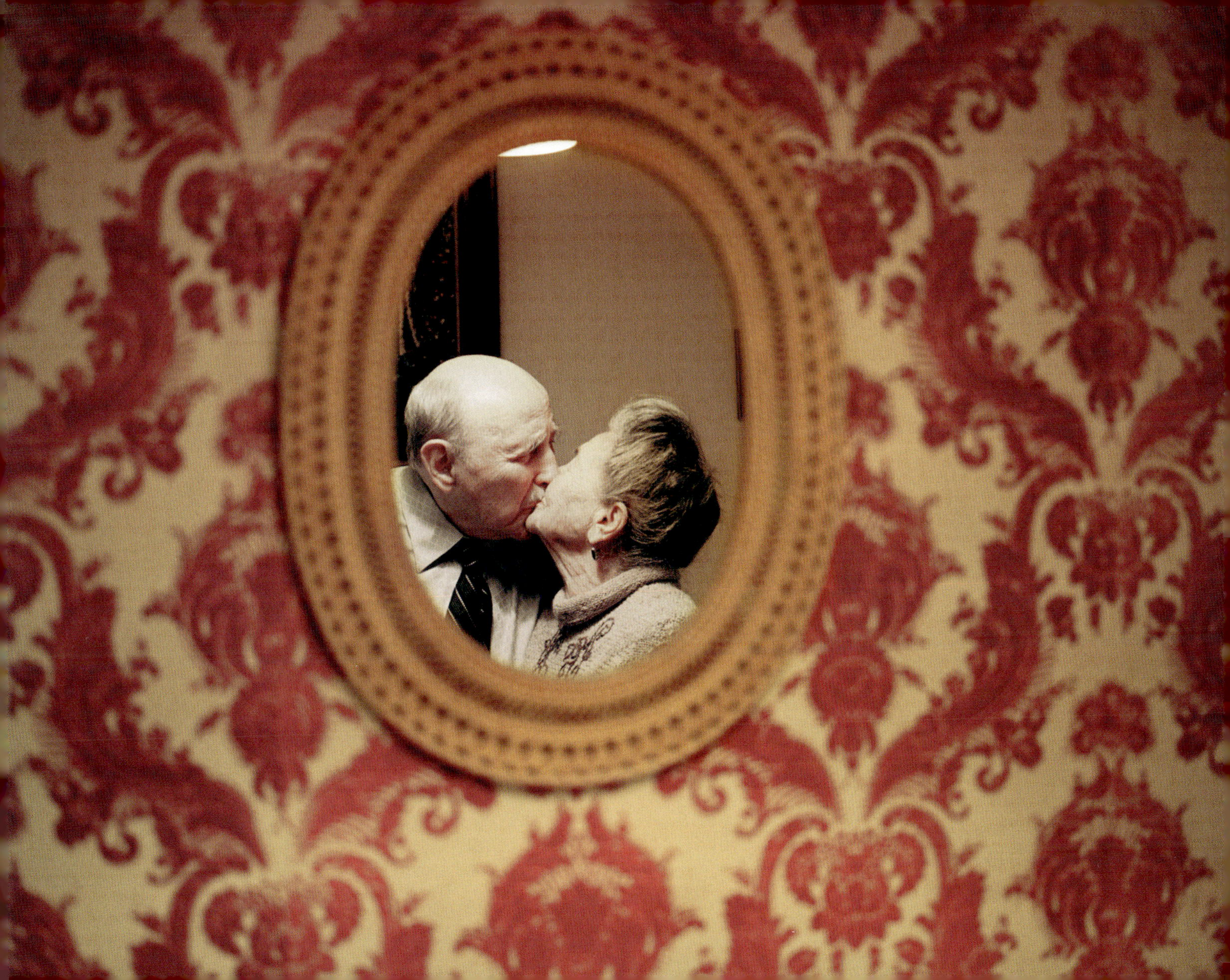

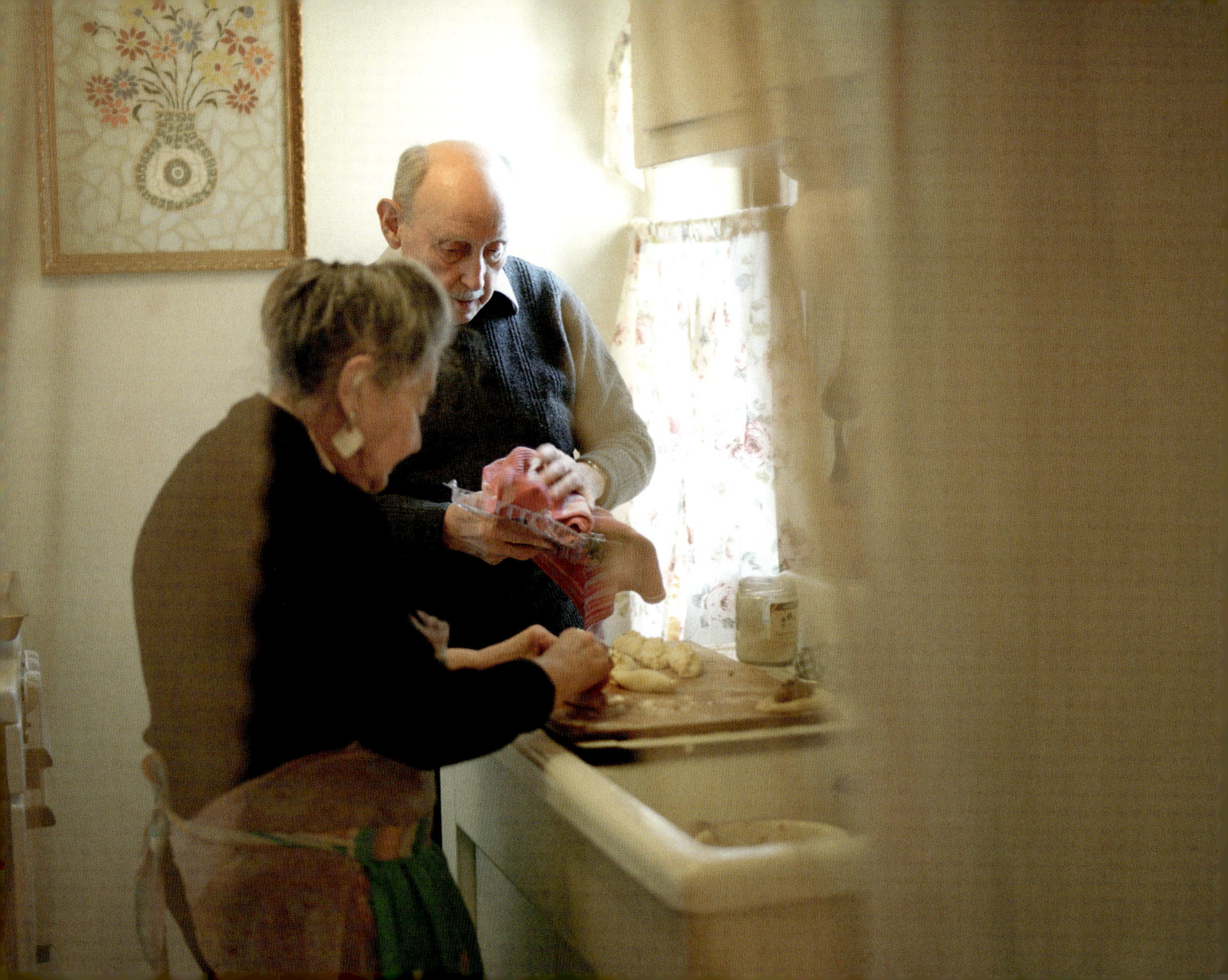

## Bob and Marcia Sparrow

Queens, New York
Married on April 14, 1957



*Bob* And I said, "Hello, you must be Marcia?" And if there is such a thing, I guess it was love at first sight. There really was an attachment. An attraction. An attraction that was unbreakable.

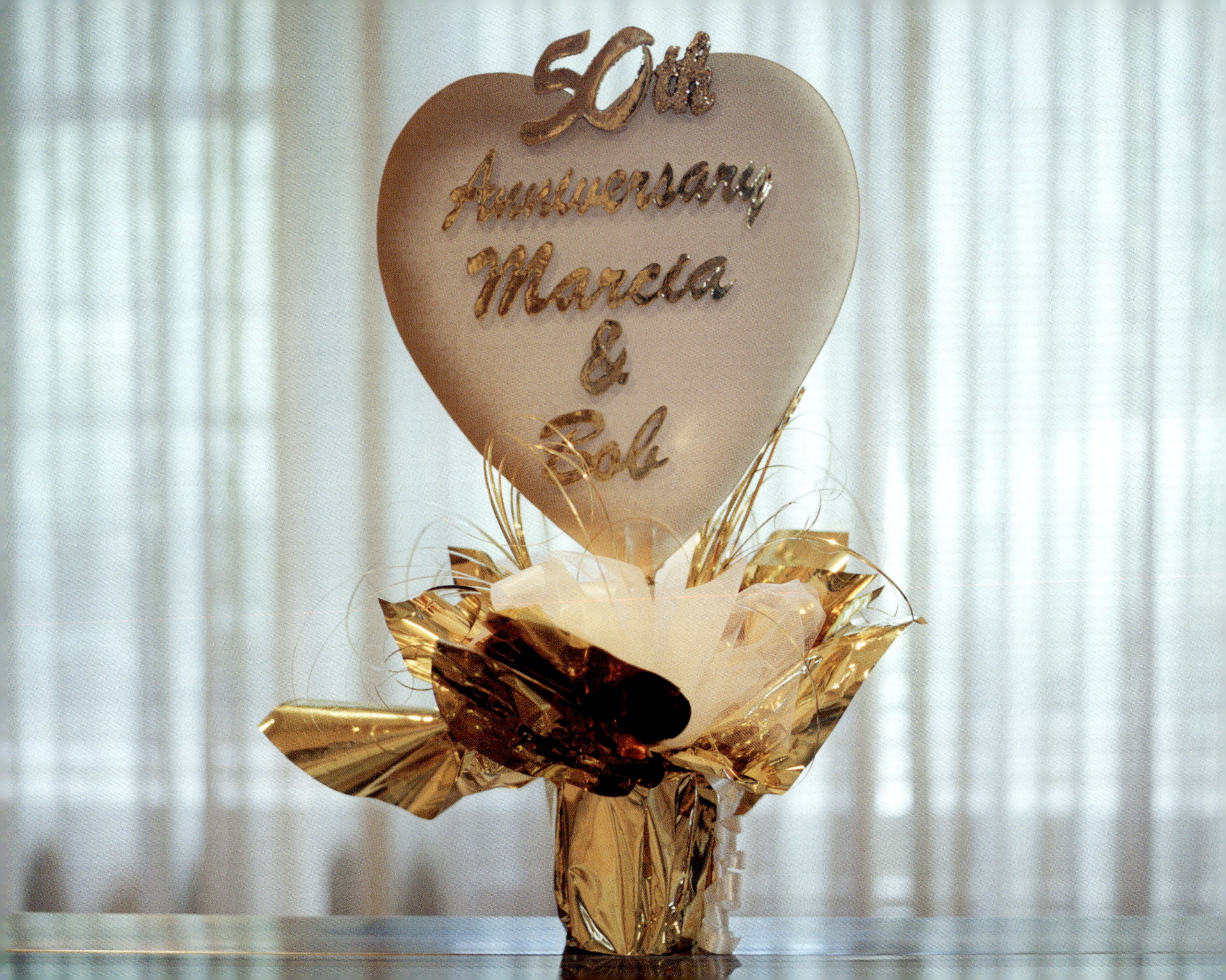
50th
Anniversary
Marcia
&
Bob

## Charles and Lillian Klein

Great Neck, New York
Married on May 30, 1940



*Charles* As children my wife and I lived in the same neighborhood, a block away, and she used to pass by the house. It was meant to be. I'll tell you one thing, living here, I only realized now what a gem I got when I married her. What a wonderful mother-in-law I had, too. My mother-in-law was my best friend, which is kind of unusual.

We've been in assisted living just about two years, but we didn't move here directly. We were in Glen Cove. We like Glen Cove very much, but the whole building was settled—it was built on a swamp so we had to get out while they renovated. We're supposed to go back in September, and we can't wait. We're looking forward to that but not too far. That's four months from now, and we count each day. Years ago, we always looked far ahead, planned ahead. When you're 97, you don't plan that far ahead anymore.

Living here, you have to live somewhere. And we wouldn't want to live with our kids, impose on them—they have their own lives to live. A year and a half, two years ago, I didn't know there was a place like this. You have nursing homes, but you never had an in-between so to speak. That's alright, but what are you going to do? Half the people here are nuts including us. I think we have all our marbles, but I know a lot of them are cracked and chipped. I know my wife doesn't. She dreams up stuff like with our 70th wedding anniversary, she thought that we were going to have a big party. We have no people left for a big party—everybody's gone.

Sometimes I say damn I'm lucky what a cute kid I married. We don't get into many arguments. It's very easy. There's two words, right or yes. So whenever she says something, I say, "Right, right, you got that right!" See, easy? Say yes and everybody's happy. I still have a little work on it, but I'm sure we'll take the rough spots out before it's over.

But we had a hell of a good one. Can't complain. We used to send out 85 Christmas cards each year—think we sent out four this year. That's the way the story goes. The story goes.

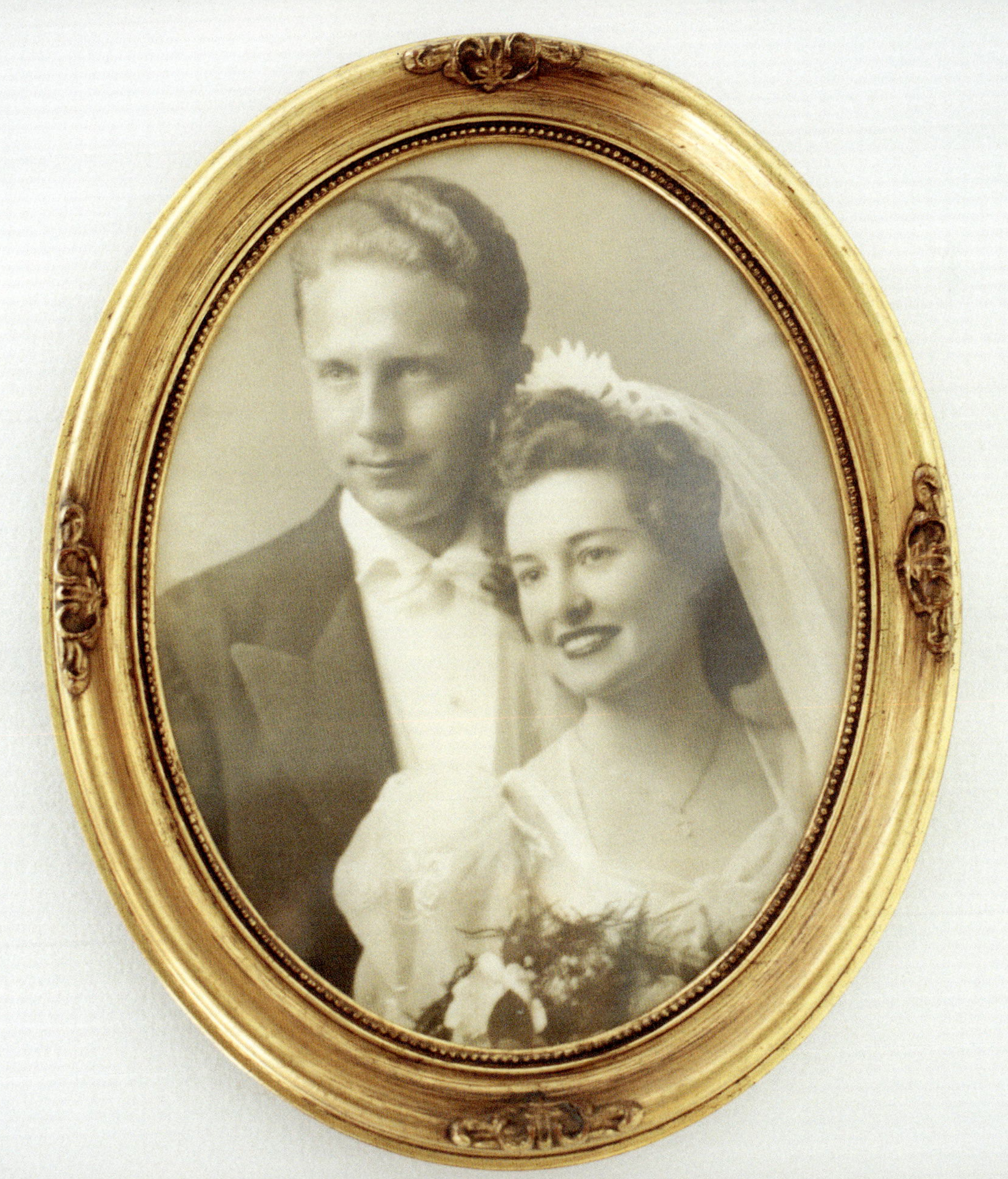

## Sheri Barden and Lois Johnson

Boston, Massachusetts

Together since February 8, 1964



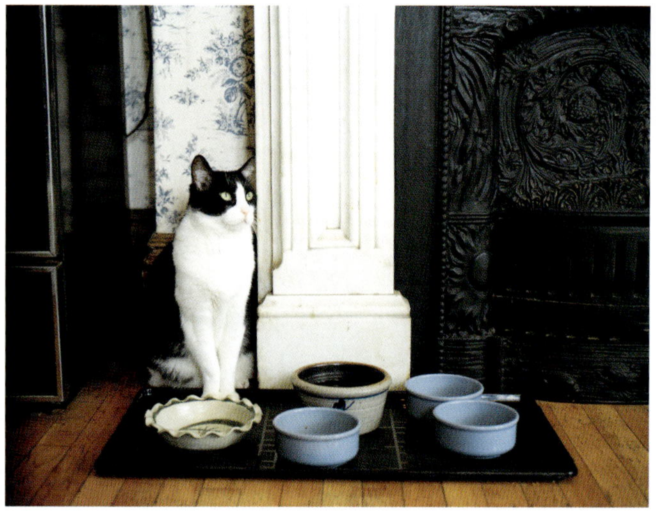

*Sheri* I don't want to live without her, and she doesn't want to live without me. I can't write a check, and she can't cook a meal. But I'm sure that straight people go through the same thing.

What I love most about her is that she never changes. In 50 years she's never been mad at me, and I can honestly say that. I used to say, "If you could only get mad at me once in a while. Put me in my place!" "Oh," she said, "but you'd get hurt." Well, yes, for a couple minutes. But I appreciate constructive criticism, but she never wanted to criticize me because she knew how hurt I'd be.

You see these movies of grand love affairs—Casablanca, Shakespeare, Romeo and Juliet. Wow! Passion in the grand scheme. They'd never make a movie of us, we're boring. We go to the market, we go to work, we love to shop. But there is a grand passion underneath that. Growing up I used to sit in the back seat of the car imagining loving someone as much as I love her. I never thought that would happen.

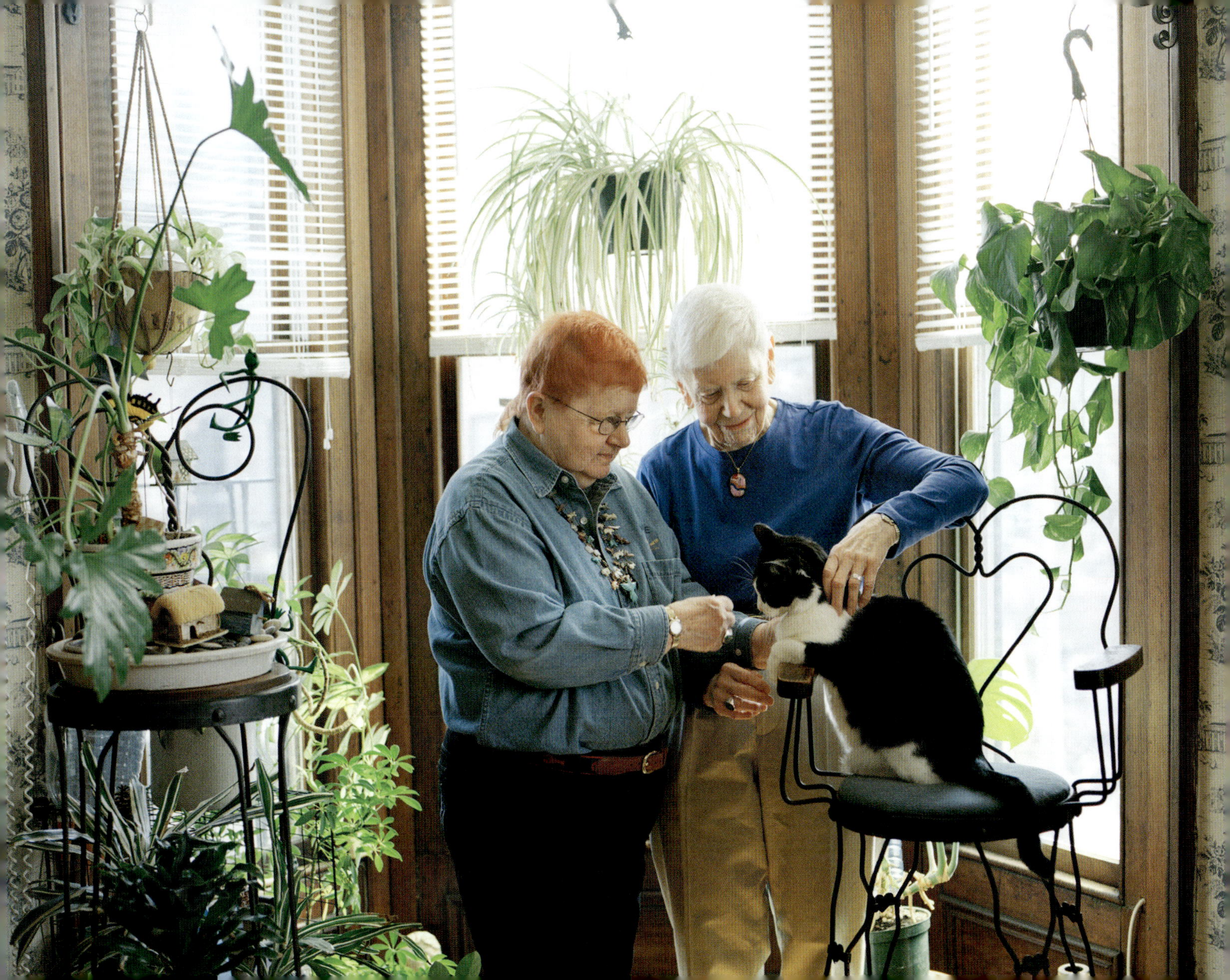

## Fortunato and Maddalena Corso

Brooklyn, New York
Married on February 4, 1941



*Fortunato* We were married on February 4th, 1941. And thank God we're together all these years! To be married, you have to love each other and trust each other. The man has to provide for the family, and you have to know how to raise your children with respect. When you have respect for your wife and your children, you teach them respect.

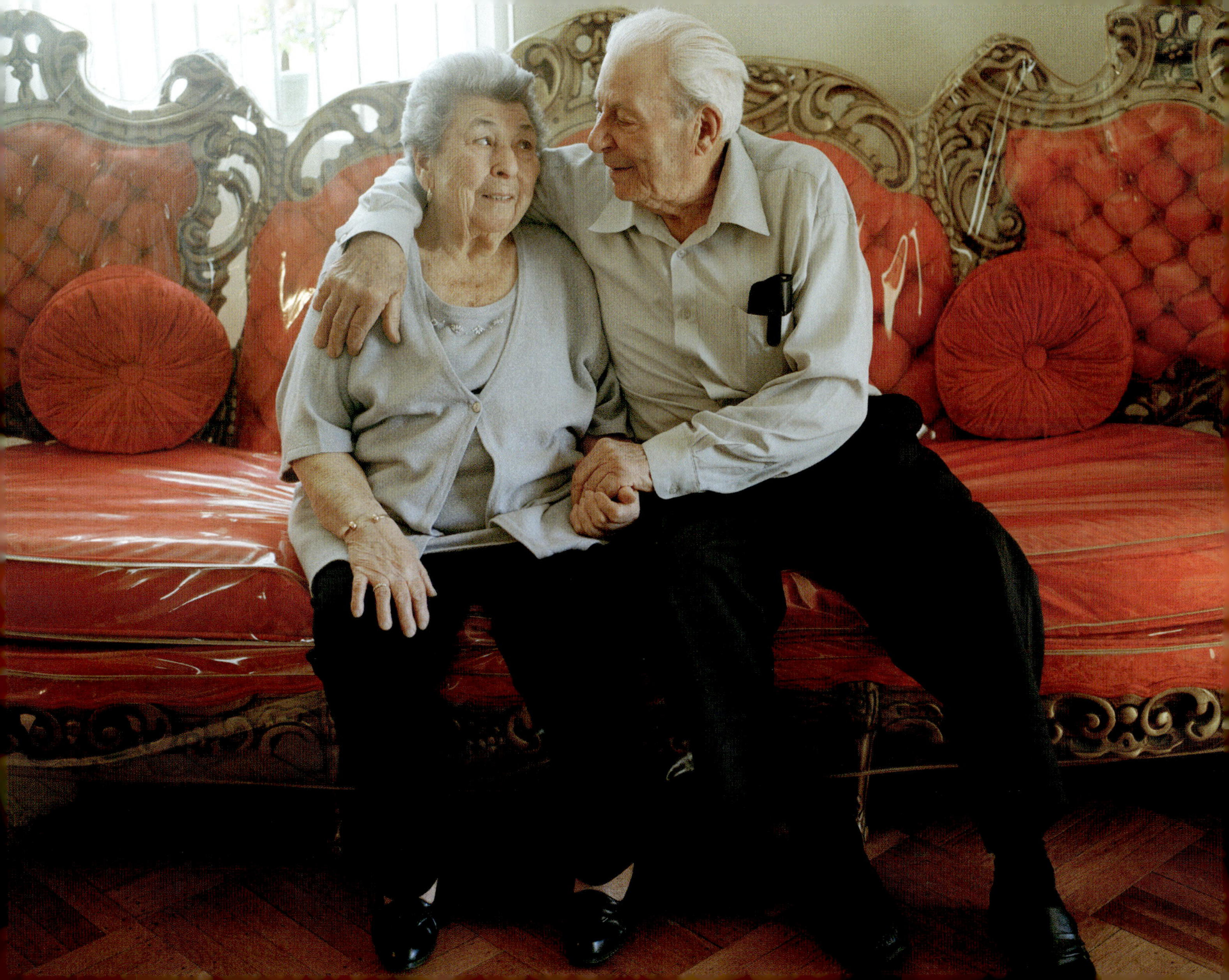

## Murray and Esther Redlitz

Brooklyn, New York
Married on February 18, 1947



*Esther* You know, sometimes I say something and he reads my mind. Or he will say, "Let's go out to eat," and that's what I had in mind. They say you sleep on one pillow you get one idea. And I think that's what happened. We think alike, we sometimes dress alike. We put out the clothes, and we dress the same way. It's the years, the years.

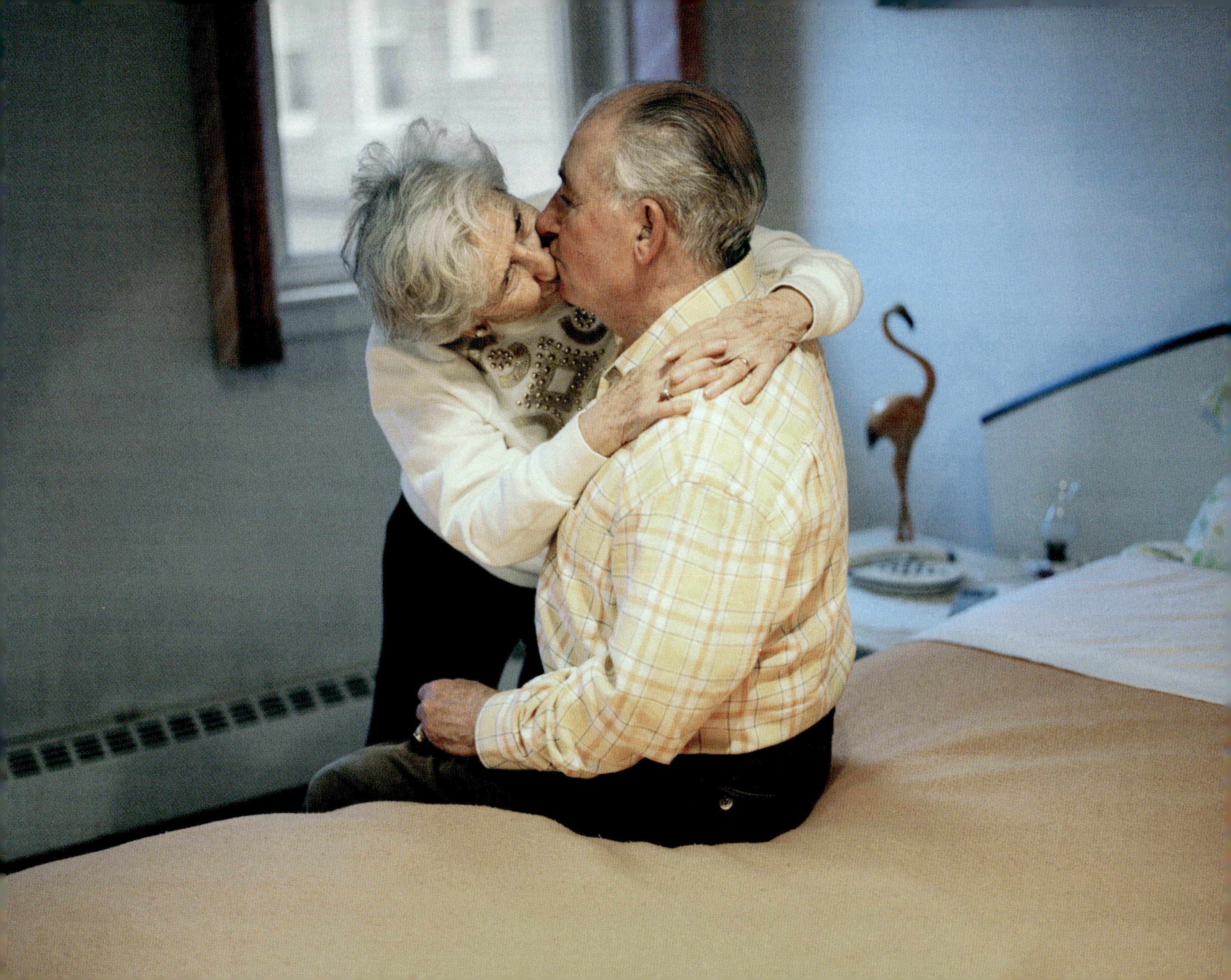

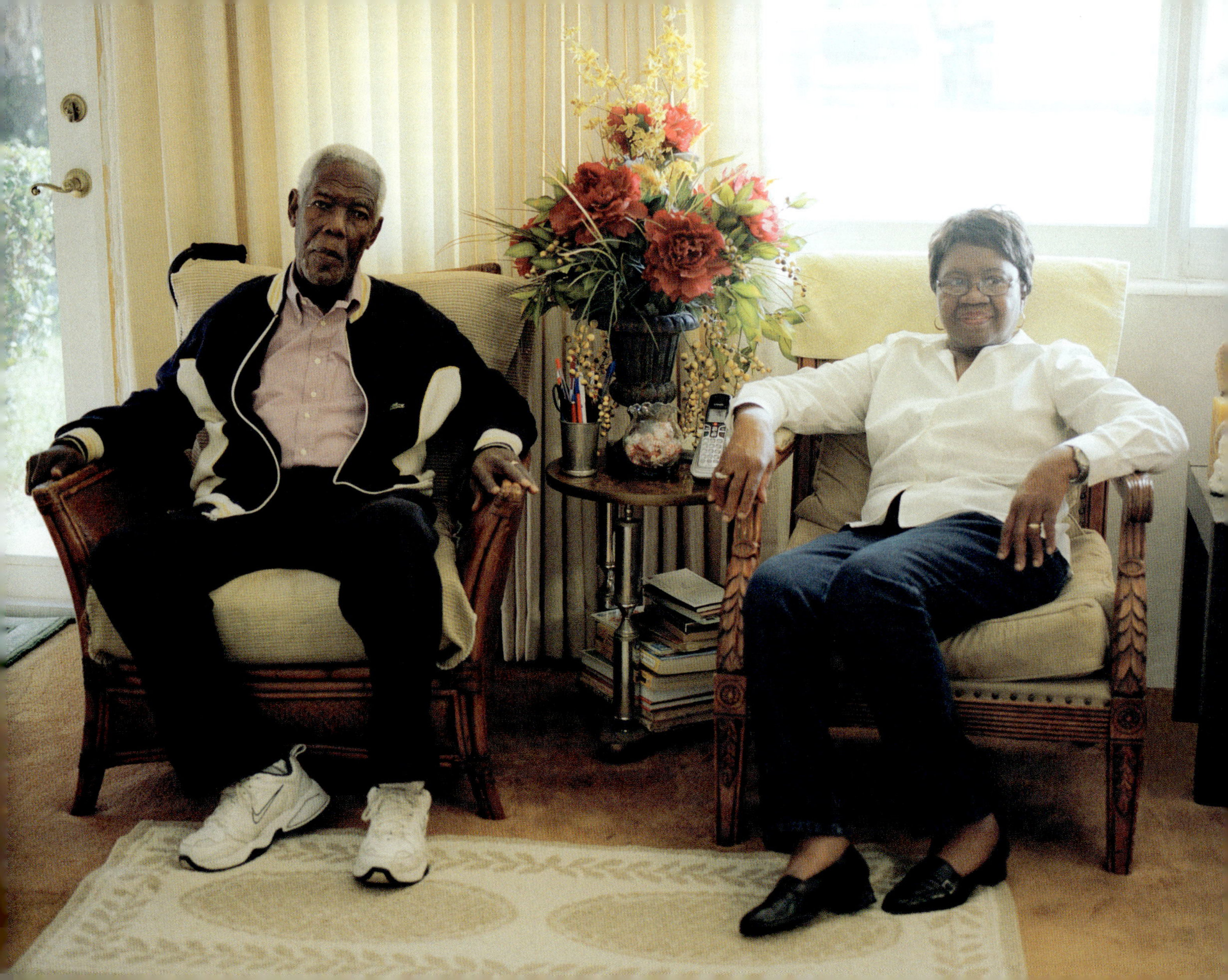

## James and Sulie Spencer

Dania Beach, Florida
Married on November 17, 1962

My name is Sulie Gooden Spencer, and we are in the city of Dania Beach, Florida. And my husband here is James Edward Spencer. I was born in Mississippi, James is a Georgia boy. We met in Florida, it was 1957. He had a sister and I had a brother down here and my brother liked his sister. That's how we got together. We dated and dated and I worked in Hollywood. I was living on premises, and I worked with the family of Robert and June Gordon and they had three children, Spencer, Johnny and Jill. And so I was the babysitter, and I did a little cooking and a little cleaning. I was there at the house full time. At that time my husband had worked for the chain food store called Food Fair. This is 50 years ago, things have changed a lot in 50 years. At that time blacks couldn't even bag groceries. They worked in the back unloading the trucks and doing that kind of work.

We got married at my church, Saint Ruth Baptist Church, and it was on a Saturday. We had a reception that night in Hollywood, and my sister was in charge of inviting people. A lot of people came to the reception that wasn't invited because that was their first chance to get to Hollywood at night without working in Hollywood. So they said oh, she intended to invite me but she just didn't. That was during segregation time, and blacks couldn't go into Hollywood unless you worked there. You had the black gardeners and the butlers—most people in that section of Hollywood had a butler, a maid and somebody to come in and do the laundry.

After we were married, the people I was working for were going to Europe, and they wanted my baby to be born before they left. So I went to the doctor for my checkup at Dr. Rubell's. He was the first of the doctors that let blacks sit in the front. Usually, the blacks had a separate waiting room. And just about everybody went to Dr. Rubell, and I knew him from the family I worked for and he was friends of theirs. So he said, "Sulie, you're gonna have the baby today." Because the Gordons were gonna leave within the next two days, they were leaving to go to Europe. So I go out to tell my husband that I'm gonna have the baby today. And he cried, "I'm not ready! You can't have the baby today, I'm not ready!" And I said, "Well, that's what the doctor said, and I have to do what the doctor says." So when Jennifer was born, it wasn't long. They induced labor, and at that time they used to just knock you out, and when you woke up, the baby was there. Jennifer was six pounds, five ounces. I thought she was a huge baby, but they said that was a small baby. I continued to work for the Gordons, and James was working there too. They wanted us to have somebody take care of the baby, and I wasn't going to let that happen, so I say well, this is the end of my job there.

So then we worked about six months for a family called the Burlingers. We worked together, James was the butler and I was the do-everything person. And when we worked for the Burlingers in Fort Lauderdale, they drank a lot. So James said, "Oh, we gonna go home early today. I'm gonna make them drunk and we'll go home." They'd get drunk and they went to sleep. But we couldn't leave them, that didn't work. So I said, "Don't make them drunk anymore." But then Mr. Burlinger passed. So for about a month I was without a job.



Then I read an ad in the paper that this lady was looking for a housekeeper. So I went for the interview that Monday and I had my letter of recommendation from the Burlingers, and they knew the Gordon family that I had worked for. They had their own company, and so she went to work and I started work that day. Now I'm making $45 a week, I'm showing off in big cotton. I still go to that house every day. The parents are dead, her son is dead. Now when I started there, the grandson was five years old, now Jeffrey is the boss. And so I go every day, I go in for an hour. He just wants somebody to come in and check the house. I think it was kinda left in the will as long as Sulie comes in she has a job.

I think there was a song one time that said love is a two-way street. Love is what it does, not what it say. Our pastor says love is an action word. You don't talk love. One lady asked me, she said, "Sulie, how did you stay married? What is your secret for staying married for so long?" And we have never had a fight. You can tell he's not going to say that much, I do the talking and you can't fuss by yourself. And he doesn't argue. And I get mad at him because he won't fight back! I mean, how can you fight by yourself? And so, I told her one thing, "The man always says he's the head. So you got to let him think he has the last word. Whether he has the last word or not, you gotta let him think he has the last word." So I think that settles most arguments.

We never slept in separate rooms because of a disagreement. Sometimes I slept with my back to him, but it wasn't that I went to another room. So we have our disagreements, but then we know how to compromise. Love isn't a lot of kissing and sex and all that. I think people get that confused with love, but love isn't that, and I think because we've been together so long I know him and sometimes I can just about tell what he's thinking and I think he's about the same way.

And so they say, did Spencer buy you any flowers for this holiday or that holiday? I say, "Yeah, he bought them but he didn't know he bought them." And so after our 45th anniversary, my fingers had gotten larger, so I said, "I need new rings." So I went and bought me a new ring. They said, "Oh, Spencer bought you a ring?" "Oh yeah, he bought the ring but he didn't know he bought the ring." So those kinds of things. And he'll say he like what I do, but he's not the one to go out and pick it out. No, he's not going to go do that. If I want something, well, you know what you like, go get the one you like. So that's the kind of thing we do. I guess he's somewhat romantic, but he's not the lovey-dovey type. He'll come behind me and hug me and say something like, "Girl, I've brought you from a long way." And I say, "Sometimes I want you to take me back!" But it's that kind of thing. Even with the children. They know Daddy loves them, but he's never been that affectionate type.

Over the years, you think of love differently. When you're younger, the way they walk, the way they talk. The way he holds my hand. But after sickness and strokes and different things, you're just glad he's able to hold your hand. That he gets up in the morning and says good morning. You begin to see love through different eyes because the eyesight got dimmer anyway. I think love is like anything else. They say wine is better with age. That's the way love is, it's better because you appreciate little things. I love his demeanor, his quietness, he's never been loud. If he raised his voice, you know, even with the kids, if Daddy yells, then all of us are in trouble. And he's never been one that's been out there, I knew where he was. When he left the house, he never went out and just say, "I'll see you later." I knew where he was going, and if I needed him, then I could say oh, he's at such and such place. I never went to see if he was there, but if he said that's where he was going, then I believed him.

We stayed in Florida, never did get to nursing school, but I think God has been good to both of us. As I say, James, he's had two strokes and he's usually a little more talkative than he is now, but he goes on dialysis now three times a week, Monday, Wednesday and Friday.

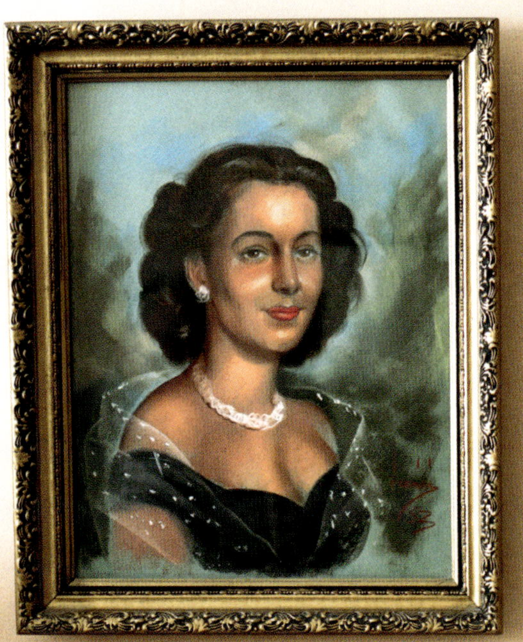

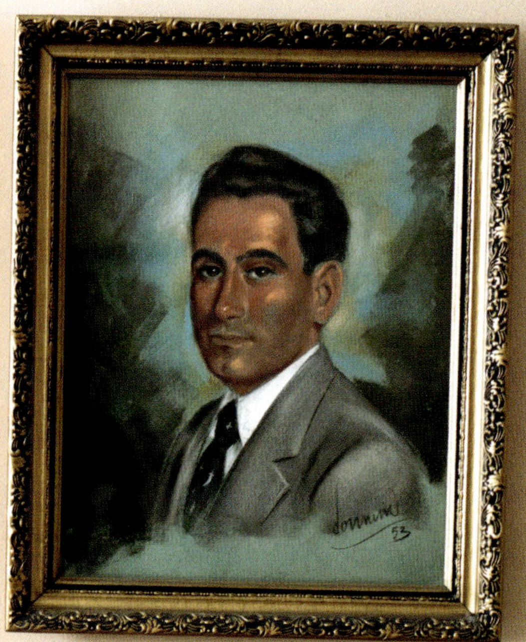

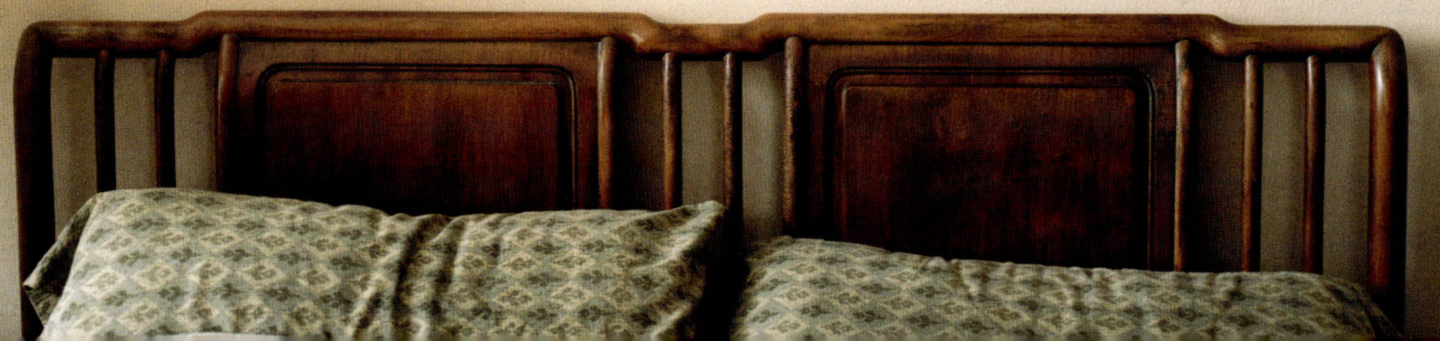

## Sol and Gloria Holtzman

Brooklyn, New York
Married on January 16, 1954

*Gloria* I'm Gloria Holtzman and this is Sol Holtzman and we have been married 54 years.

*Sol* An eternity!

*Gloria* An eternity!

We are here in Brooklyn, and we've been living in the same building for 54 years except in two different apartments. First, we were in a three-room apartment. And then after our oldest—we have two daughters—after the second one was born, our landlord did us a favor, and he put us into a two-bedroom apartment which we are even in today.

We met 56 years ago at Bay 2 in Brighton Beach where a lot of young people used to spend their weekends and their summer days. I don't know just who's around there now, but I know it exists. And Sol, you were with your friends.

*Sol* We had a group of young boys...

*Gloria* And I was with one of my friends, and it was just a matter of talking to each other because we were on the beach, on the sand close to each other. At the end of the day, I think that I offered my phone number rather than waiting for him to ask for my number.

*Sol* You didn't offer. You gave!

*Gloria* See, I gave it. And not having a pencil or paper, I wrote it on a matchbook cover, which in those days all of us had them because a lot of us did smoke.

*Sol* I had the matches in my pocket and one evening we were hanging around and one guy said, "Hey what about those girls down at the beach?" I said, "Oh, I have a phone number!" I called and we made a date.

*Gloria* Well, now I gotta tell you a really funny story about that date. I was the kind of girl, with most of my friends, that when we went out on a Saturday night, Sunday mornings we were busy on the telephone telling each other how our dates were and I was the kind of girl that I fell in love right away. So the next day, I would tell my friend, "Terrific, I mean, I'm in love already." But after the first date with Sol, I did not feel that way. I told my friend, "No, he was very nice. We had a good time, but that was it." She was the one that came back with the statement, "I bet this is the guy you're gonna end up marrying!"

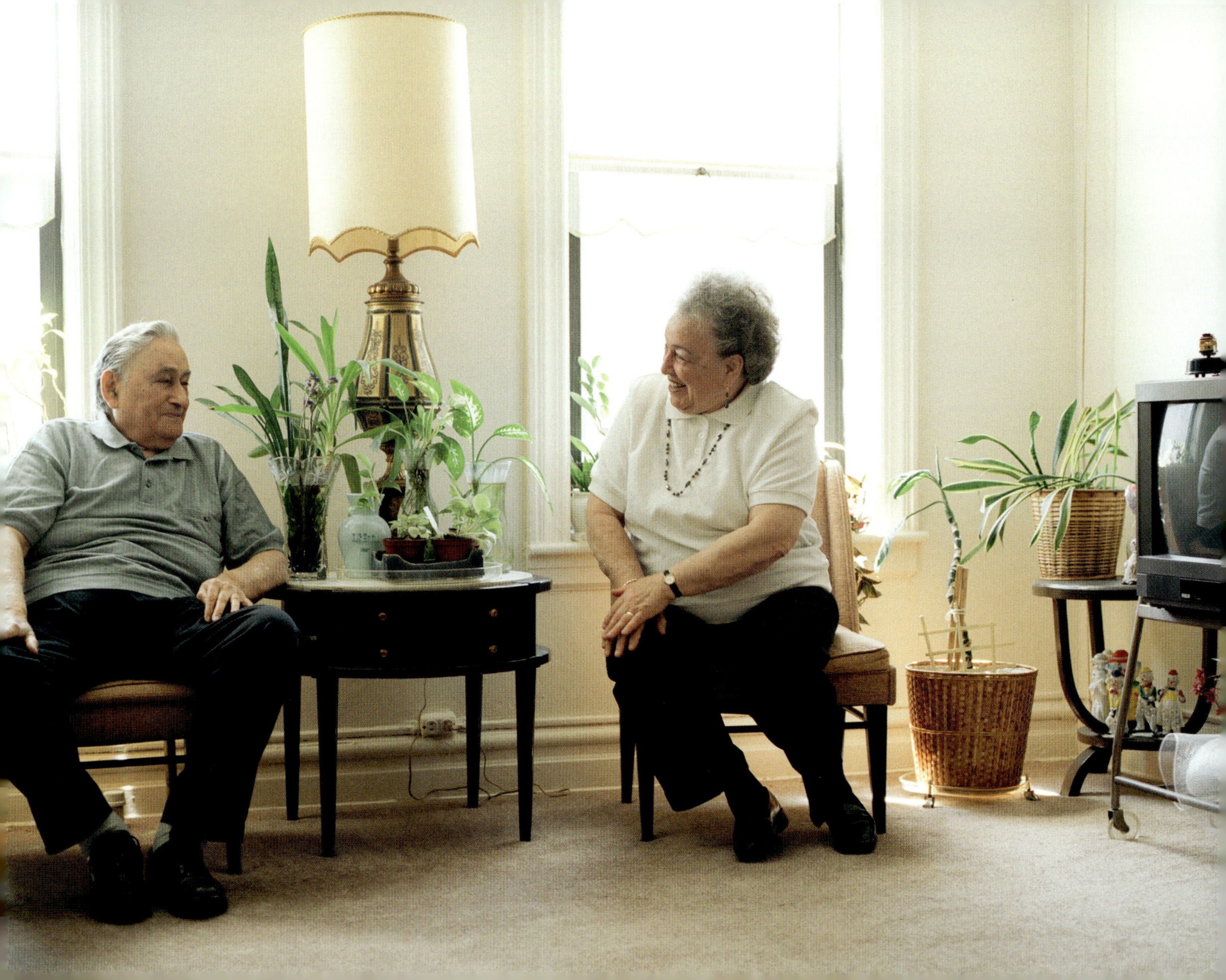

I think it only proved to this day that you can't judge right away. As you get to know a person, love comes. That was what happened as far as I was concerned. We got to know each other, and we ended up getting engaged.

We have our arguments. We have our ups and downs. We're human. We have our likes. He likes some things and I like others. Sol likes to do a lot of reading. The only thing I read is a newspaper.

*Sol* How could you read a newspaper? You're always on the telephone.

*Gloria* It's true. I like to socialize on the phone a lot. Sol always used to comment that I could see somebody all day, my friend or something, but in the night, I could still speak to her over a half an hour. But I think that's women and girls. I like to talk to people, and I like to find out about how they are. I am interested in knowing how people are feeling.

Obviously, you have to marry a person who has similar likes. See, when you're younger, you do more together. I think when you get to my age already the tendency could be where he may do things he prefers. Like now, I think he looks forward to the day I go to work, so he can do his own thing. And it's reading. Pretty much reading.

*Sol* I always said that she was not necessarily the only one that I could have gone for. There were numerous girls that I felt that I could have gone with and gotten along with it. Just so happens that this is the one. Well, actually, she forced me into it! She ran after me, and I couldn't get away.

*Gloria* Oh no, I don't remember that at all.

*Sol* Well, you gave me your phone number!

*Gloria* Well, that's to start with.

*Sol* I was never gonna get married. I didn't have a job. I was hustling jewelry, and I was making a lot of money but I didn't have a job. My mother complained that I wasn't married and wasn't working. So I took the post office test, and I figured I will go for two, three months and then I'll quit. Three months wound up 30 years.

*Gloria* One thing I know, he was older and he was a more mature person than the other guys I was meeting up with even though he was not financially in a position like some of the other guys I might have met. He was a nice-looking man, too. Boy! He was easygoing. With me, I don't know, I was boy crazy.

## Bernard and Leila Weber

Little Neck, New York
Married on February 12, 1950



*Leila* I think that as I matured, and I certainly had many years to mature, I'm a better wife now than I was. Sometimes I would get angry. Now I don't. I say, isn't it silly? I would sometimes in my youth say, "Stop talking." I don't do that anymore. I think that I am a better wife as I aged than I was at the beginning.

When we got married, my mother gave me $1500, which was a lot of money at that time. And she said, "Now you plan your wedding and anything you want to buy has to come out of this $1500." So I went to Rothman's Inn, this old dilapidated place, and you had to walk up the steps and it was five dollars a couple. I borrowed a wedding gown, and that's what we did. We lived with my mother and father for two and a half years. We were three girls in the family, and my mother always treated us like princesses. I never did the dishes, I never made the bed, I never cooked any meals. But I always went to work. When it was time for me to have our own apartment, I was able to do everything. I worked, cleaned, cooked. Took care of the children when they came. And gone was the princess.

I'll still get dressed and say to Bern, "How do I look?" He says, "You look beautiful! You look lovely!" Which is such a nice thing to say. I realize how many years we have lived and enjoyed and been together, and I am grateful for them. Bern has given me a wonderful life. And because of the fact that we're structured, busy people, we know how to live and to live with each other. Bern kept to his job 41 years with the police department. He ended up a deputy inspector. I was a teacher in the New York City school system for 31 years, and I became an assistant principal. We have two sons, and they were both very good boys growing up. We didn't expect too much. We didn't demand too much. We saved.

*Bernard* I would say in today's age we were married very young. I was 23 years old and Leila was 21, just out of college. Whatever it is attracted me to Leila—it may have been her legs. I was a leg person. We met and got to know each other and felt comfortable with each other. I took the police exam earlier, and I didn't know how I made out. And all of a sudden the letter came for me to come for a physical, and I became a policeman because now I met my future bride. I had to earn a living.

We once were asked the question, "Why is this marriage a success?" It comes down to knowing that she's here. We help each other. I had help from Leila with all the problems that I had, including the police department. I came home, told her about it, she calmed me down. In essence, maybe I was able to just express it. She was my sounding board. And she would give me back the answers, tell me what she thought.

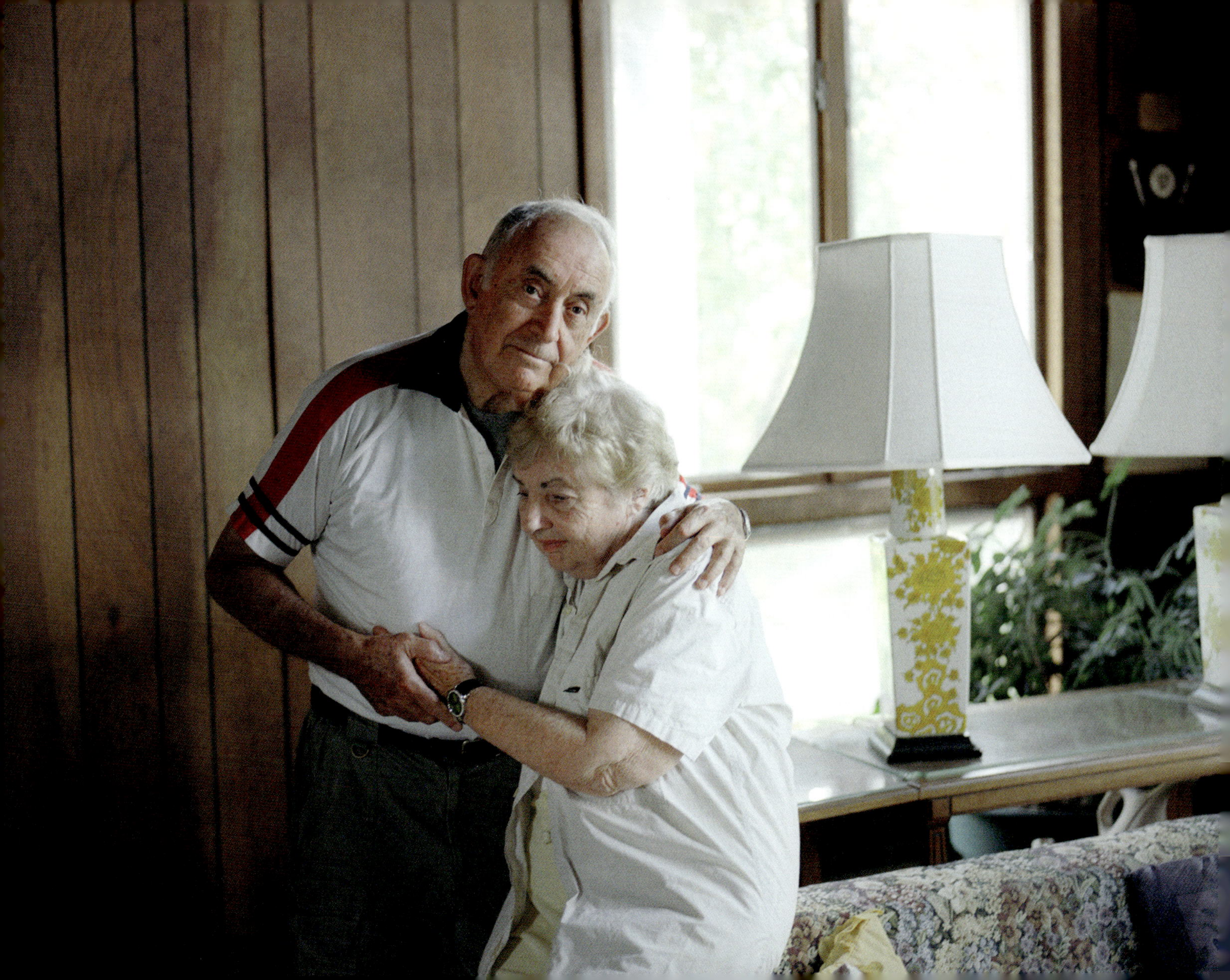

## Ralph and Mary Lou Peak

Boise, Idaho

Married on December 22, 1952



*Mary Lou* It's so easy to say I love this, I love that. And I love you. You say that to your children, you say it to friends, you say it to your husband or wife. So there's all kinds of love, but what does love really mean? It means trust, it means respect, it means security. You're willing to share not only your body but your deepest thoughts and feelings with someone else. If you've been in a relationship and you get your heart broken so to speak, it's very difficult to start over and trust someone with your feelings again. I was 26 and Ralph was 27 when we got married. So we had both been disappointed in experiences with the opposite sex.

*Ralph* Yes, indeed. When the Korean War started, I was in the Army Reserve and was ordered back to duty. I left my wife and two children behind, and she filed for divorce.

*Mary Lou* Because she got involved with somebody that she hired to paint her house.

*Ralph* So that was the beginning of the end of that marriage.

*Mary Lou* So anyway, he learned a lesson. And that's the reason why I say trust is so important. If I'd ever given him any reason to distrust me, he would have been out the door like a shot.

*Ralph* Oh, I don't know about that.

*Mary Lou* You were kind of addicted to me.

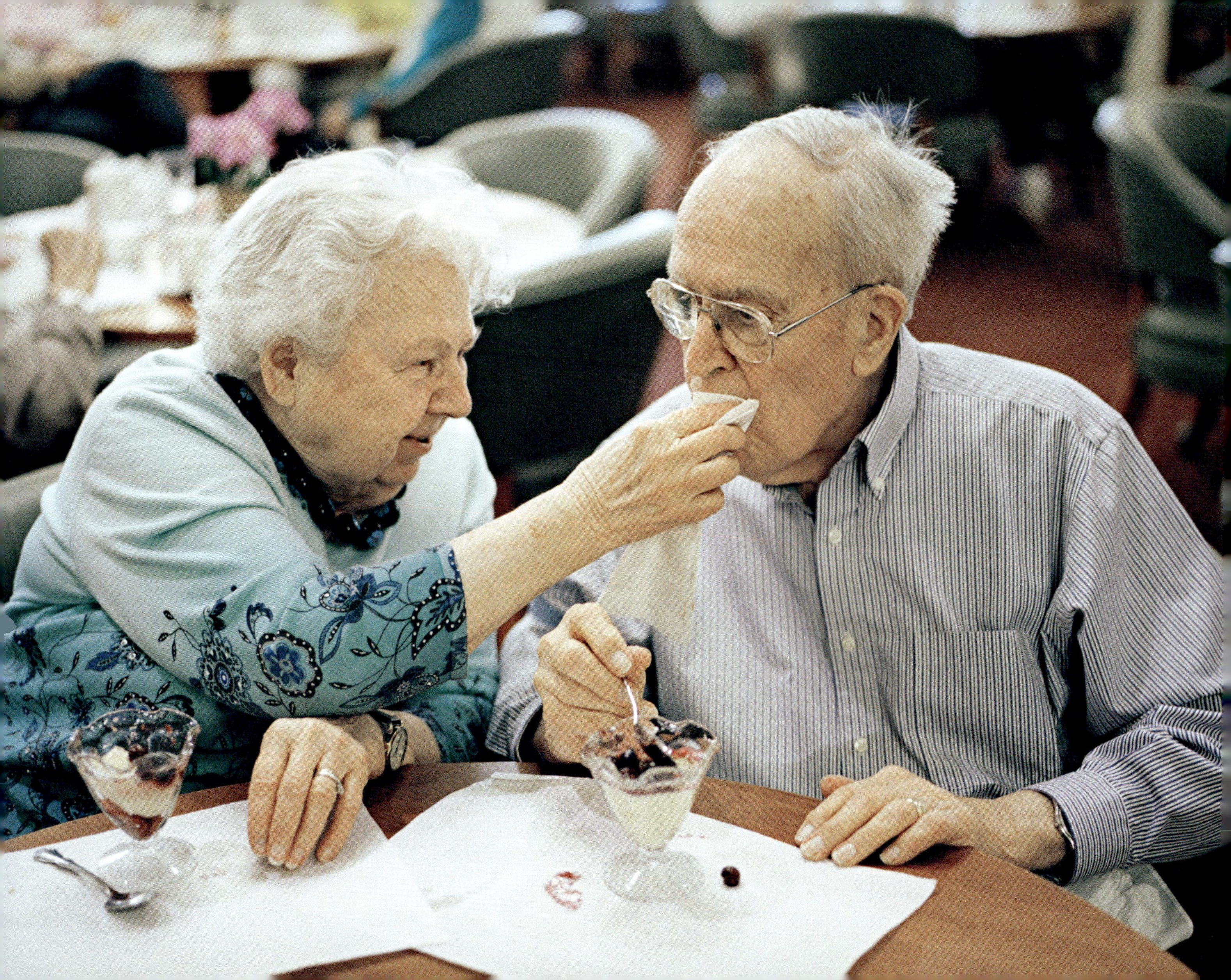

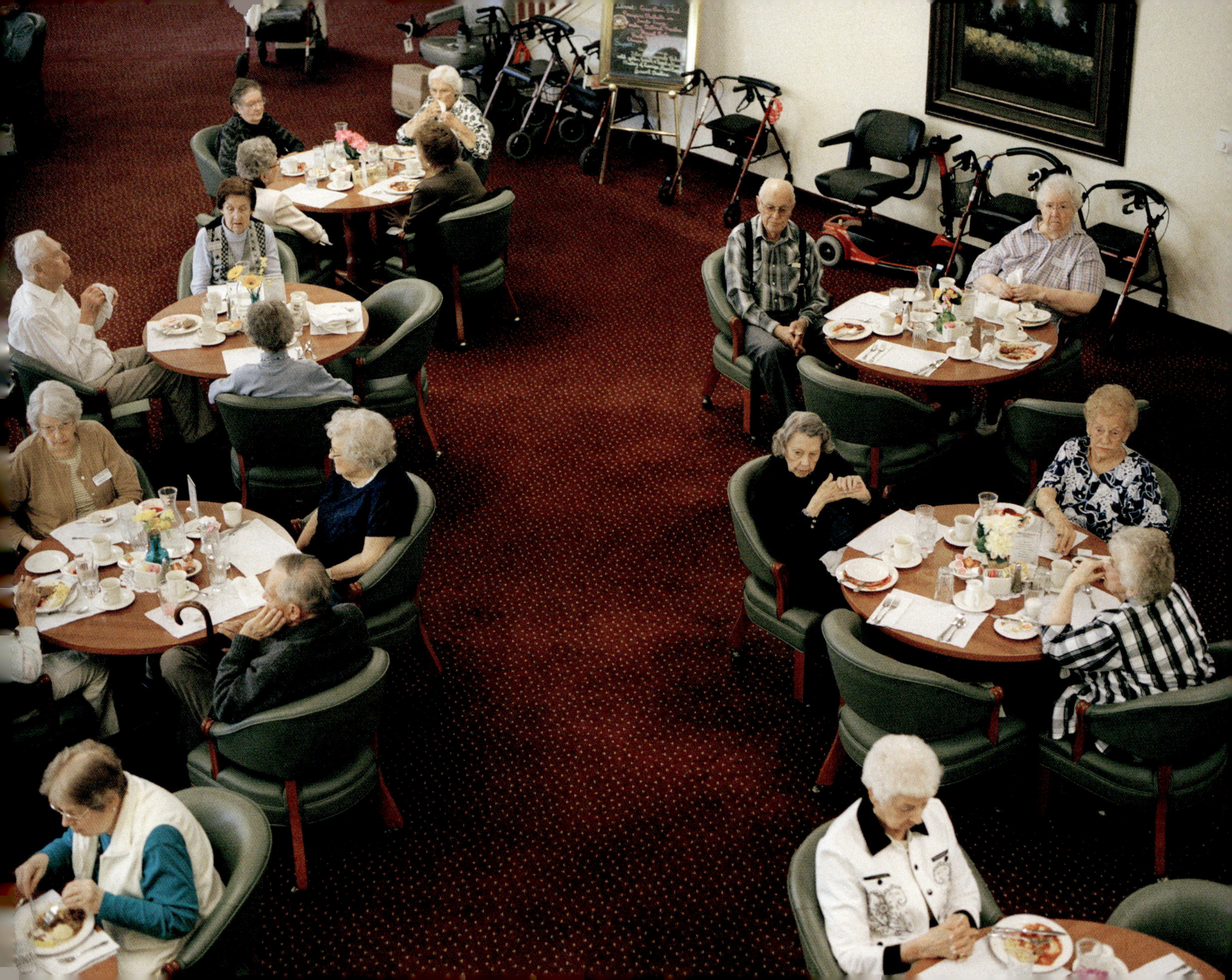

## Samuel and Grace Goldstein

Brooklyn, New York
Married on December 15, 1951



*Grace* My family objected to me marrying Sam because they felt that I didn't know him well enough. But I felt in my heart that I knew him. And there was something about me, maybe because I am a Libra. I had a feeling that he would be a good husband, a good friend to me, a good companion. I knew of many people who didn't marry the person they loved because of family objections. And I thought that isn't going to happen to me. Because if I didn't meet anyone equal to him, I would always hold it against my family. But if my marriage failed, I had only myself to blame.

When we go out Saturday night or on weekends, I still feel like we are dating. We'll go out for breakfast Saturday and Sunday. And I look forward to it because we're dressed, we're out, and it's not like, well, I'm too lazy right now to get up, get dressed and go out of the house. We get up early. As a matter of fact, we go to breakfast and we know the people already because the same people go to breakfast, so it's like a nice reunion every Saturday and Sunday.

I take pride in myself, and he takes pride in me. I'm not ashamed to introduce him to anybody, and I noticed that he's not ashamed to introduce me. I'm 80 years old, but nobody wants to believe it. I exercise. I go to Bally's fitness center, and I make sure I am always properly dressed. And I have good color combinations because many people compliment what I wear. I put on my makeup, I set my hair, I comb it, so I can always look proper. I haven't neglected myself, and this is one of the things that people should not forget. Women, in particular, because men don't have to set their hair, and they don't have to wear makeup. Women do and I don't think they should neglect themselves regardless of age, regardless of how many years they are married.

We go for vacation to Spain, and we get up and dance. We're called the dancers. We're lively, because a lot of people that come to Spain are European and they are more low-key, more old-fashioned in their ideas, and they can't believe that we are still getting up and holding hands. But this is the way we are. Even at night, when we go to bed, we hold hands. Yesterday, he had a dinner meeting, and I was beside myself. It's very lonely when you have companionship for so long, someone to have dinner with. But I knew he was coming home. So that was a very warm feeling. I guess that's one of the reasons why we look after each other. We want one another to be around for as long as possible.

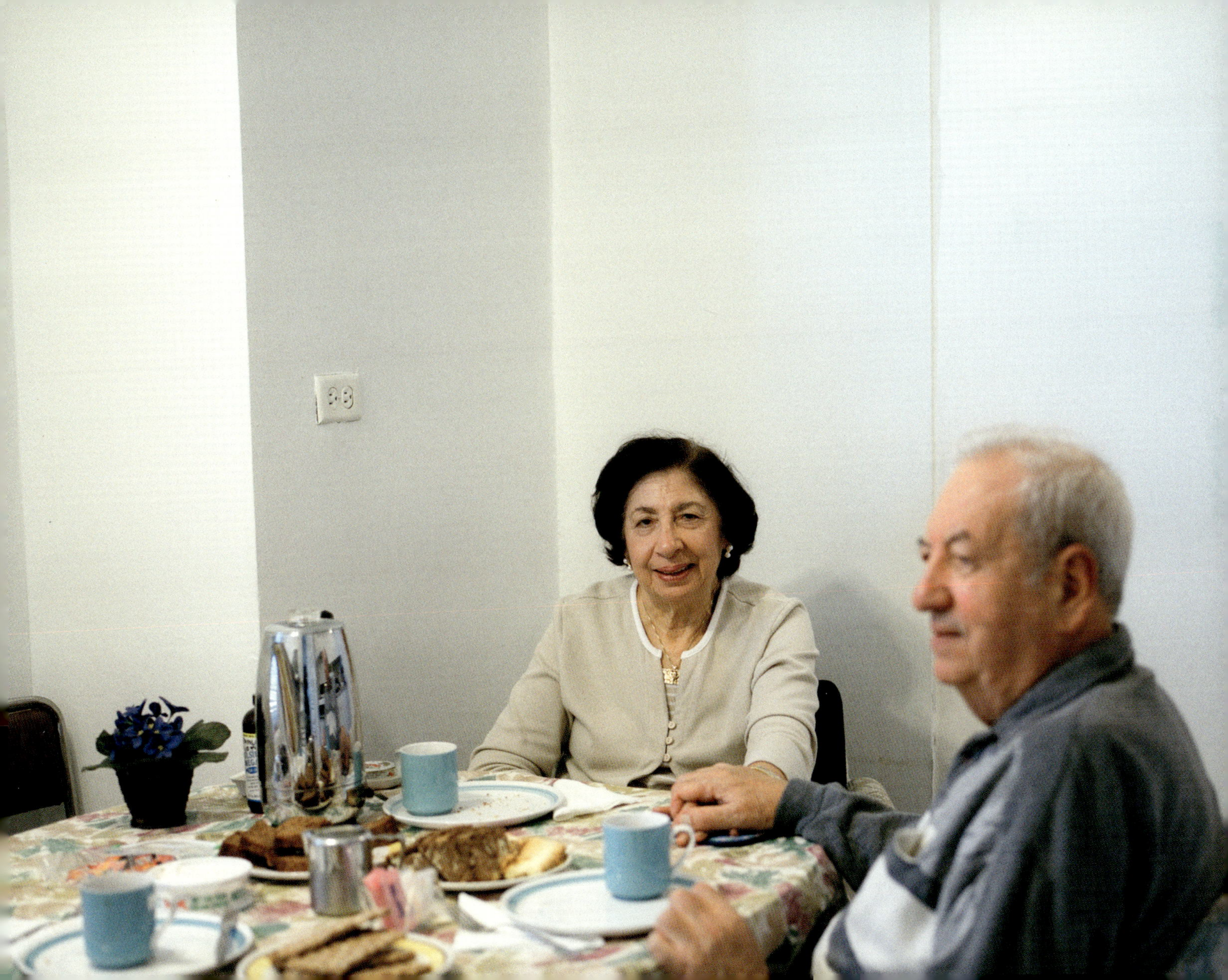

## Yaakov and Mariya Shapirshetyn

Brooklyn, New York

Married on July 6, 1949



*Yaakov* What is the secret to love? A secret is a secret, and I don't reveal my secrets.

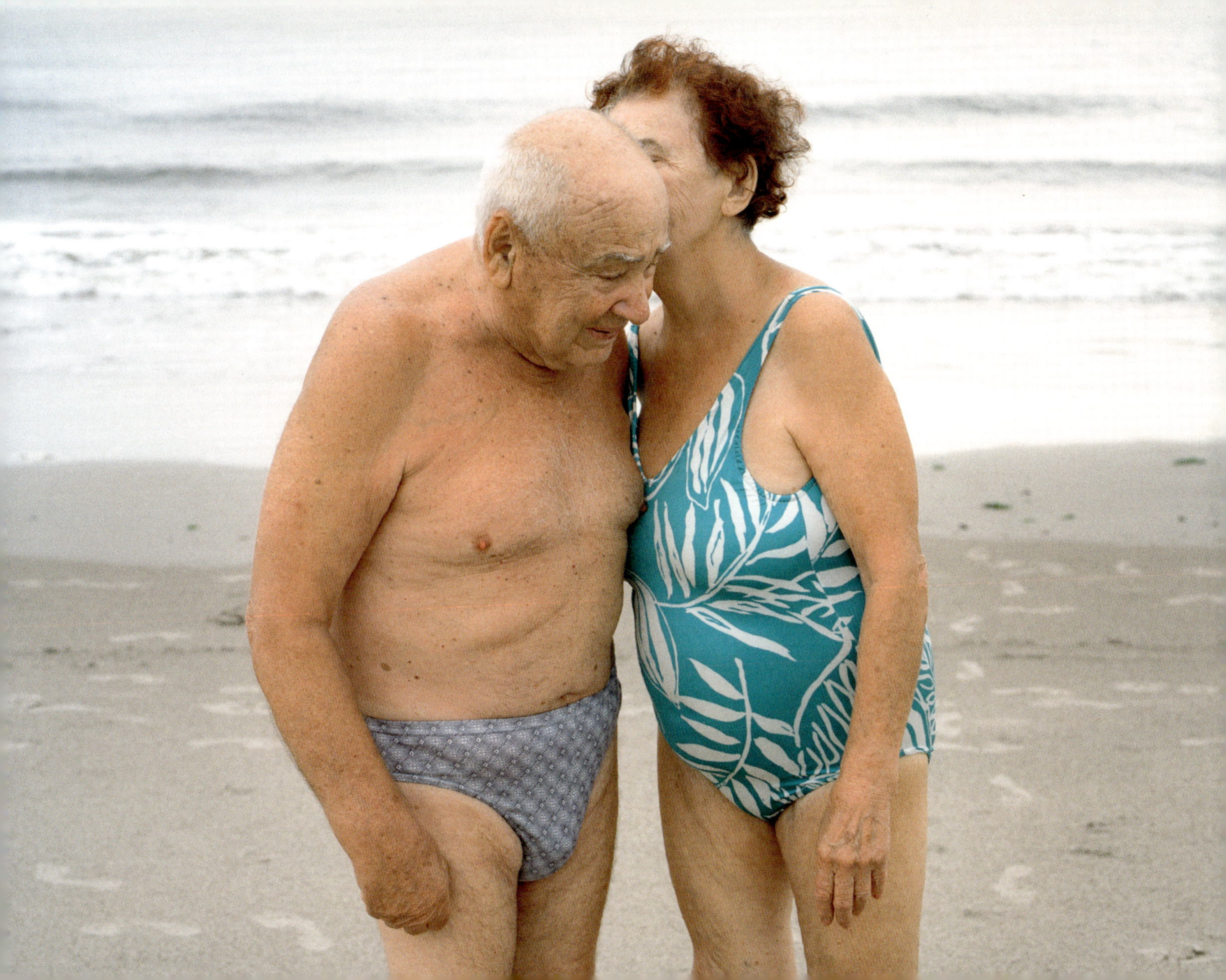

## Dick Dehn and Gary Payne

Fort Lauderdale, Florida
Together since September 2, 1957



*Dick* I don't know when we suddenly said we were in love. It was not instantaneous.

In gay life, long-term relationships back then tended to be a week or a month, and that's what we kind of expected. Everybody's too fickle. They always think that there's something better across the street. I don't know why we were different, but once we got together, that was it.

We've been together 56 years. A couple of times I've thought, yes, I've known him longer than I knew my mother. And my mother died in the early '80s. I've known him, and he's known me longer than anybody else on this earth. I never regretted it. I don't know just exactly what love is, but he was the person that I wanted to spend the rest of my life with and we have. To us, love meant that we did not want to be apart. We built our life on each other.

I have really flowered under him. I was a very shy, cautious person. And through him I changed my life completely. I did fairly well at work. I was an engineer, and I just don't think that I would have gotten the promotions without him. He encouraged me. He certainly did change my entire personality.

Many years later, after I retired, we bought a motor home. And we lived in the motor home, and we had no other place to live. We just traveled. We were way up in northern Minnesota, and we had a big fight. And he got up and went out and said, "I'm going." He got in the car and drove away. And an hour later he was back, and he said, "I had to go to the bathroom." And he came in, and that was the end of that fight. So we've had, I won't say monumental fights, but we have had fights. But we have never left each other for more than a few hours.

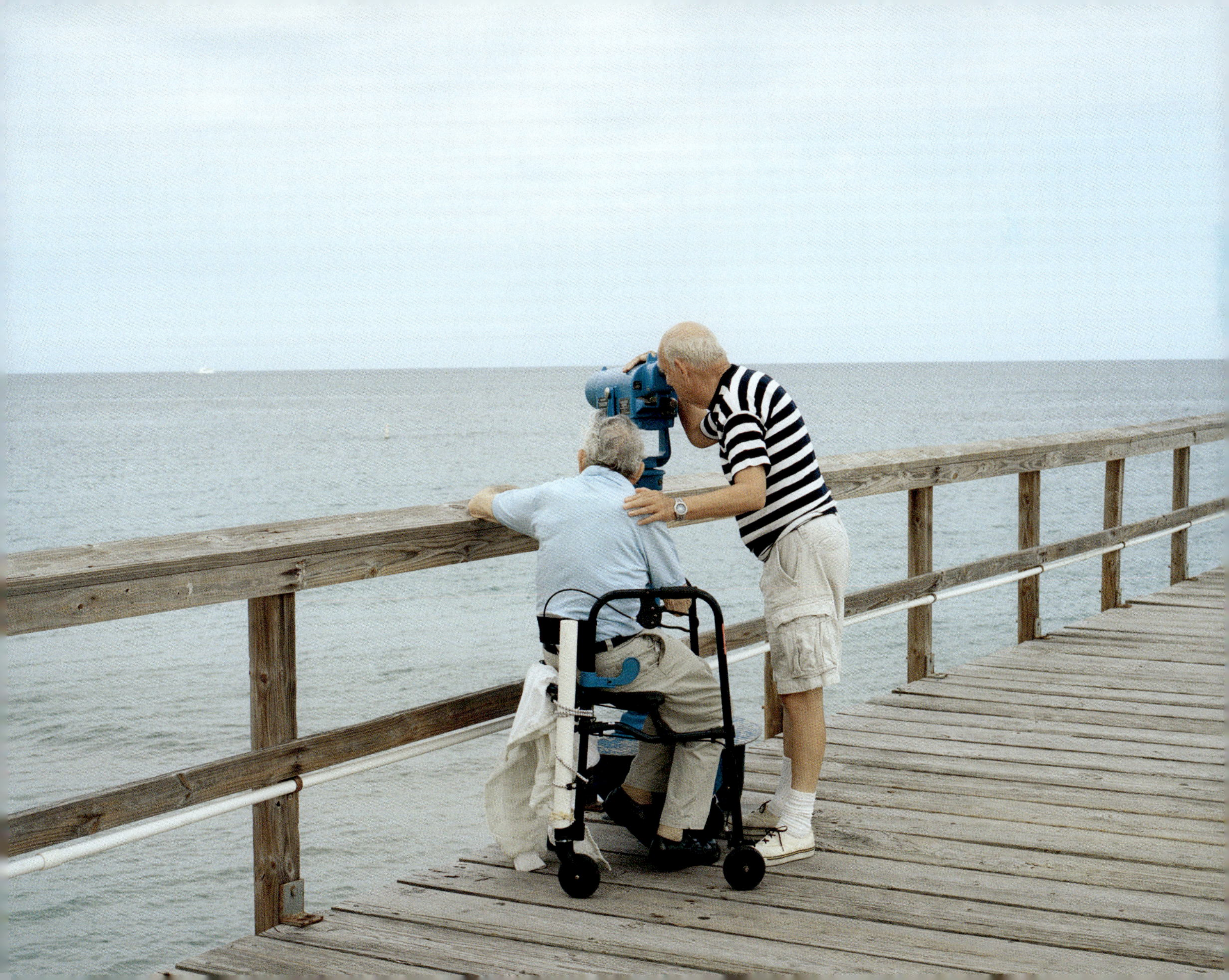

## Felice Stamegna and Santina De Fabritiis

Itri, Italy

Married on April 29, 1948



*Felice* We fell in love in Fondi, Italy. It was from Fondi that I was taken by the Germans to Monte Cassino. I was hardly given anything to eat, but they made me work despite everything. I was always a farmer. I met my wife on the farm after the war.

As farmers we hardly had any food at that time. Everybody who used to come to my house would say, "You are farmers and you have nothing to eat?" During the war everything was destroyed. We were able to arrange ourselves with various other farmers by trading fruits and vegetables. I was always together with my wife.

I knew her for only five months before we were married. How did I know she was the right one? A priest had told me if you find the right woman, you will know it. If she is not the right woman, keep away. I had faith. And on Sundays if I don't go to church and attend mass, I watch it on television.

I was 24 years old when I married her, and she was 18. My father had 1000 olive trees in Itri. We used to make our own olive oil. After the war the olive oil was not how it was once upon a time. We used to pick the olives from the tree by hand. Now everything is done by machine.

When you get married, you only want to see the most beautiful things in the person—nothing bad. I saw everything beautiful in her—everything correct. If your wife doesn't agree with certain things, that's when marriages are broken. The youngsters today don't understand the meaning of married life. In my time everything was different because we were able to agree with each other. Even if we didn't agree, we were still able to carry on, and that made our marriage beautiful. Marriage is like the government. The government keeps changing, and marriage among young people keeps changing too.

Young people today are no longer interested in looking after farmland. I used to wake up at five in the morning, but farmers are used to this type of life. Farmers' work is not easy because it means getting up very early and either planting or picking or clearing, and we were always working all day long, both of us. I've lived all my life believing. I'm a great believer.

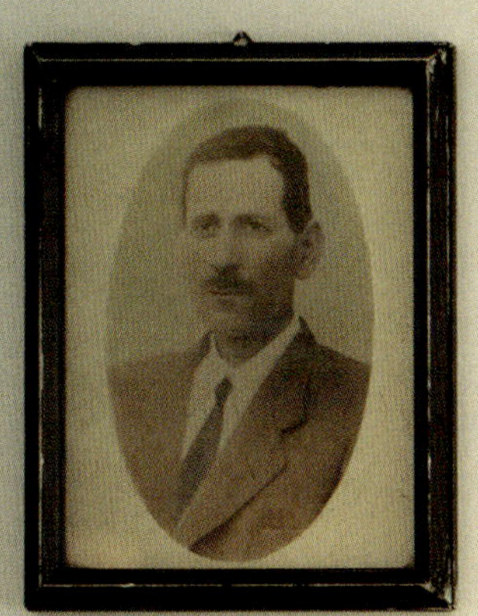

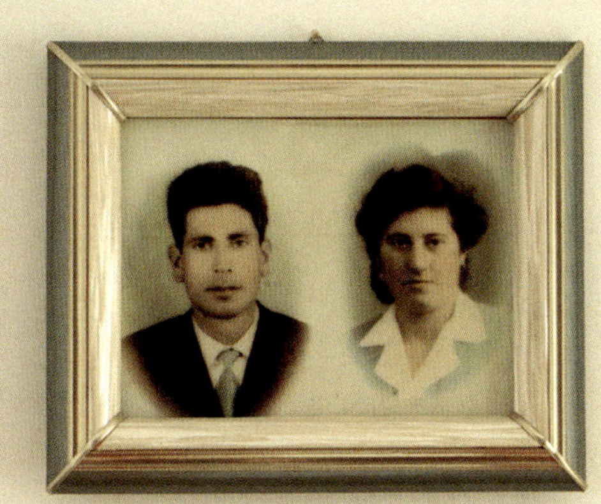

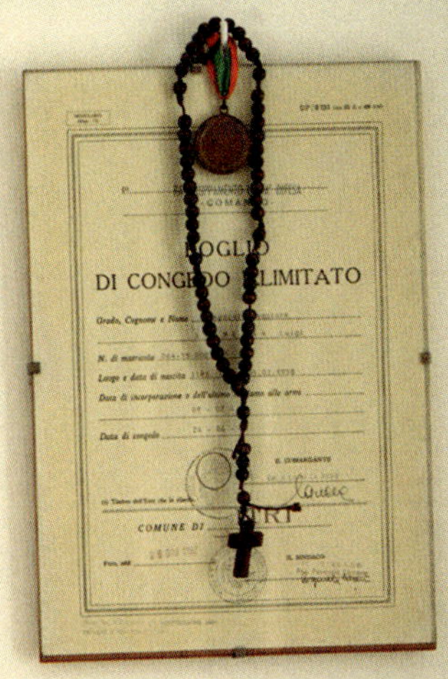

OGLIO
DI CONGEDO LIMITATO
COMUNE DI

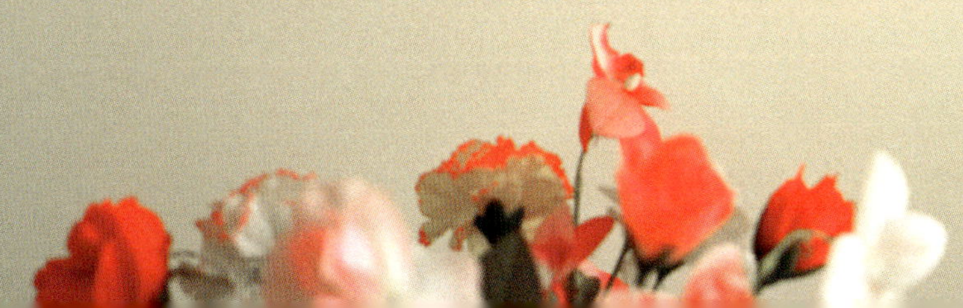

## Gabriel and Christiane Delfanti

Pierrefeu, France
Married on December 12, 1959



*Christiane* I was a nursing student at the psychiatric hospital when we met. I was 18 years old. Gabriel worked as a blacksmith. In our village there was a blacksmith who made a little bit of everything. That profession has disappeared now because tractors have replaced horses. This was during the post-war years, and it was a little archaic, old-fashioned and not very modern.

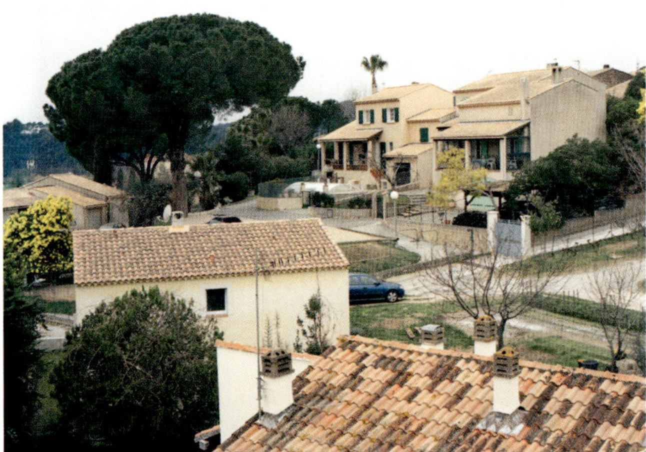

We decided to get married, but before we could, there was the Algerian War. Gabriel left for 28 months, so we had to wait for his military service to end before we could be married. Unfortunately, there was a disaster in Fréjus, at the Malpasset Dam, which gave in and flooded the entire city. And it rained here, which is uncommon, for more than 30 days in a row. The dam swelled and the dikes gave in and we got married in complete sadness. No flowers, no friends and no way of transportation.

At that time it was fashionable to get married. If it were now, we would have lived together before marriage, but the times demanded that we get married. There was no birth control, and we believed that we should not consummate the marriage until we were married by a priest. So here we are. We were fortunate enough to have a nice apartment that was well decorated and furnished. We worked with small means but not big requirements.

We've adapted our personalities. We made concessions to get there. When you are young, you dream about the perfect man or about the ideal woman. In youth, everybody dreams, we are all dreaming. A life for two is beautiful when you get along well.

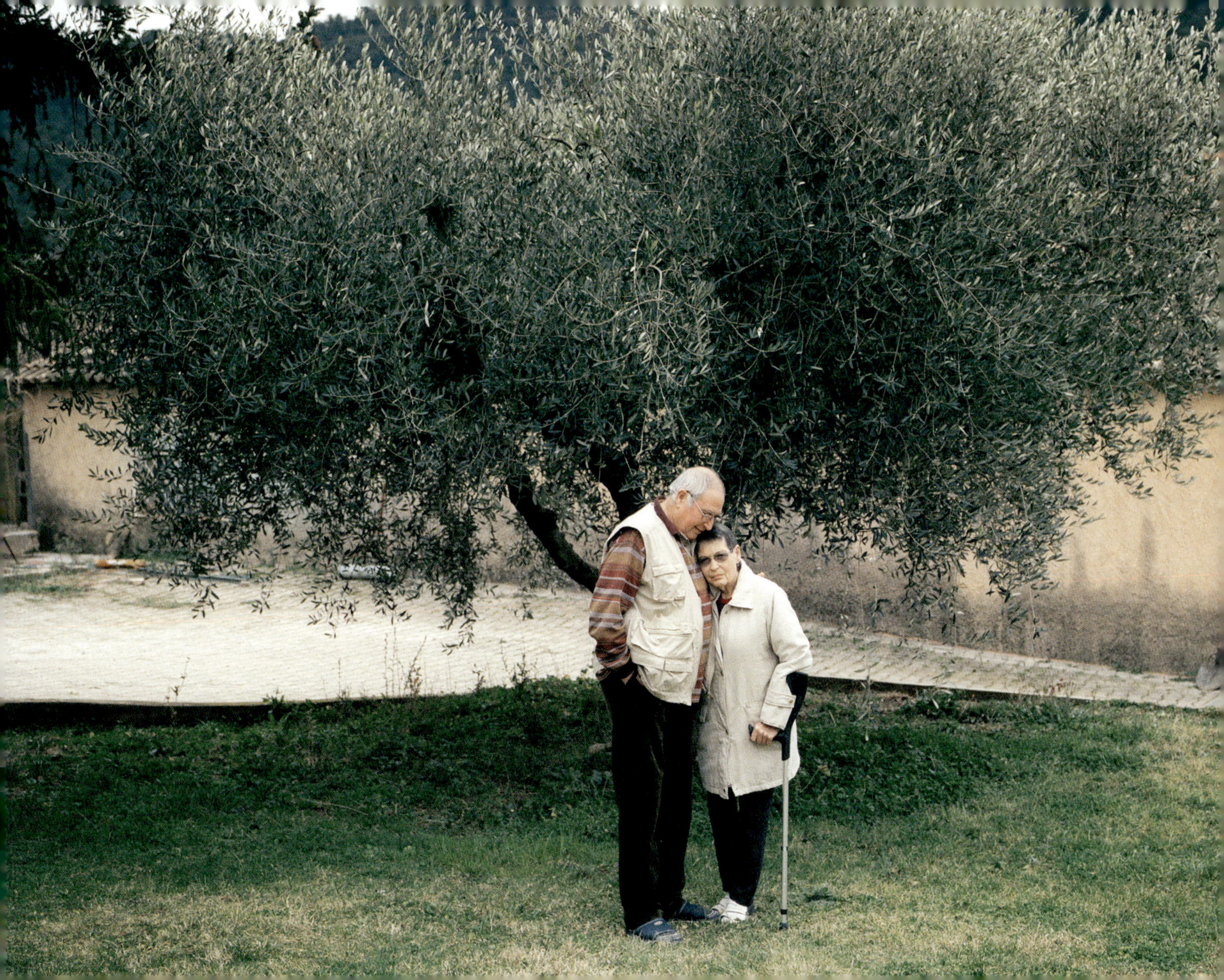

## Mehmet and Kevser Uşaklı

Çamlıbel, Turkey
Married in 1949



*Kevser* How did we meet? His sister married my brother. Then his father liked me. Mehmet liked me already anyway. He hadn't completed his military service yet, so he was saying that while he is away they would let me marry someone else. But I waited for four years for him while he was in the military. Then we had our wedding.

*Mehmet* When Kevser was born, I asked her father's permission—"Uncle Ahmet, can you give this kid to me?" "Maybe I would," he said. But it worked out well, thanks to God. Then we paired. It's been 60 years.

We got married in 1949, and in 1950 we had our first daughter. We were working hard as farmers. We seed, we harvest, we reap, we hoe. In the 1960s we were lumberjacks. We were preparing the wood and the pine trees. I did this for three years, and I had my social security. Ten years ago we didn't care about social security. We thought I had veal from this cow and that would be my social security. We also had some sheep. And then I had a cataract in my eye. If we had insurance, we would have gotten good rates. This cost this much, that costs that much. So we paid the premiums. A man from Istanbul offered us his help and took care of our social security. He asked my daughter to prepare some paperwork, and we did it.

*Kevser* Thanks to God, we took care of it.

*Mehmet* So 10 years ago we had our social security. We had three daughters. They got married. We gave our land in exchange for six apartments and gave three of them to our kids and kept the other three to ourselves. So this is our financial situation.

*Kevser* It was well. It was well.

*Mehmet* We did well. The secret is to work and help each other. To raise our kids and see them in good places. I wrote it down, where they come from, how many kids they have, so that it can all continue. They had their own kids, so we take care of the grandkids now.

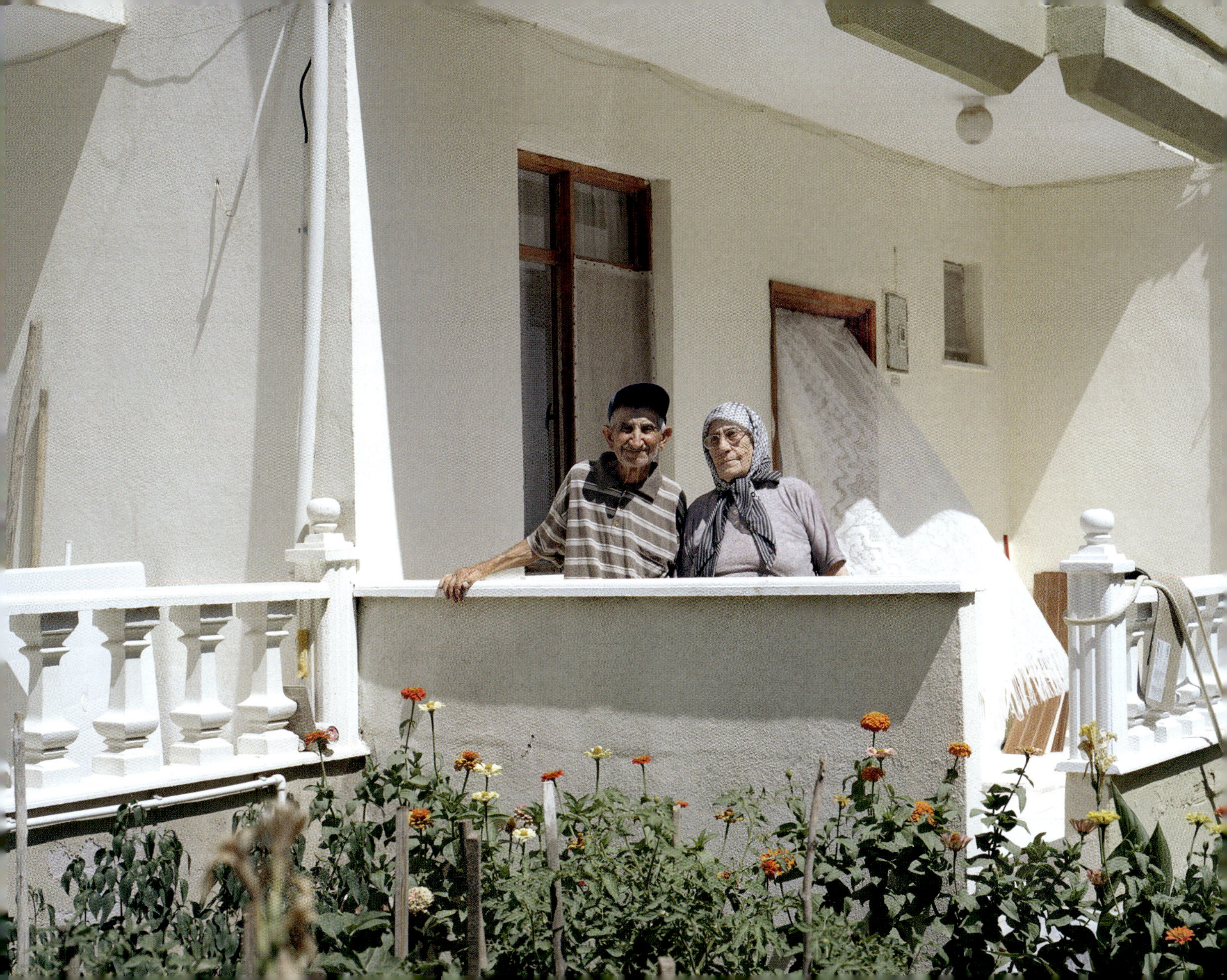

## Aldo de'Spagnolis and Maria Filiozzi

Itri, Italy

Married on October 23, 1949



*Aldo* When I first saw her, she was 14 and I was 22. Was there a concern that she was too young for me? No! Even now I look like a young child! Yes, even now I'm still young.

This was a fierce love. At that time her dad wouldn't let her meet me because he thought she was too young. My father went to speak about her to her father and she was barely 16 at the time and her father said, "She's only a baby!" I would serenade her at night from her window with the song *C'è una Chiesetta Amor.* This became our song.

We were married in this house. My father built the entire building and left one floor each to me and my four brothers. We had a small altar between the study and the bathroom and more than 200 people came. We were married after the war, and at the time no one went out. Everyone remained in their homes. We've lived in this apartment all our lives and still have the bedroom furniture our parents gave us.

We've almost become like young lovers again. We're just one. Even if we don't show it openly, as time goes by, we are more than ever one. The affection is always there. All I want is to always be close to my wife.

*Maria* I am a very anxious person. I always think something unfortunate will happen to the people I love. I was very young during the time of the war, and I had many friends who died under air raids. This influenced my personality a lot. I also lost my mother at 22, and I live with the nightmare of losing the people I love, including Aldo.

I am jealous of him because he is very funny and positive, and every person that meets him is fascinated with his beautiful character. Sometimes I'll cry if he speaks to another woman.

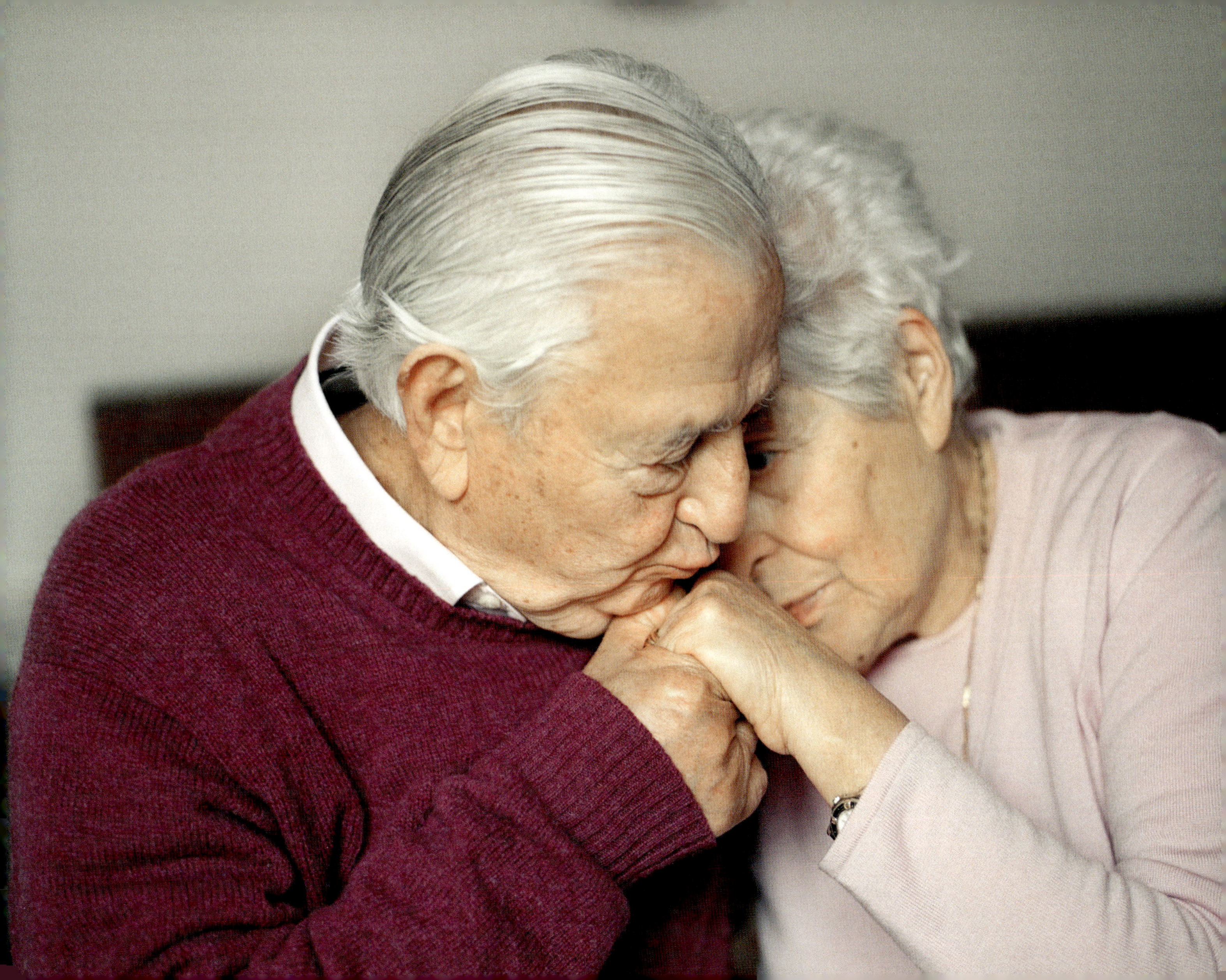

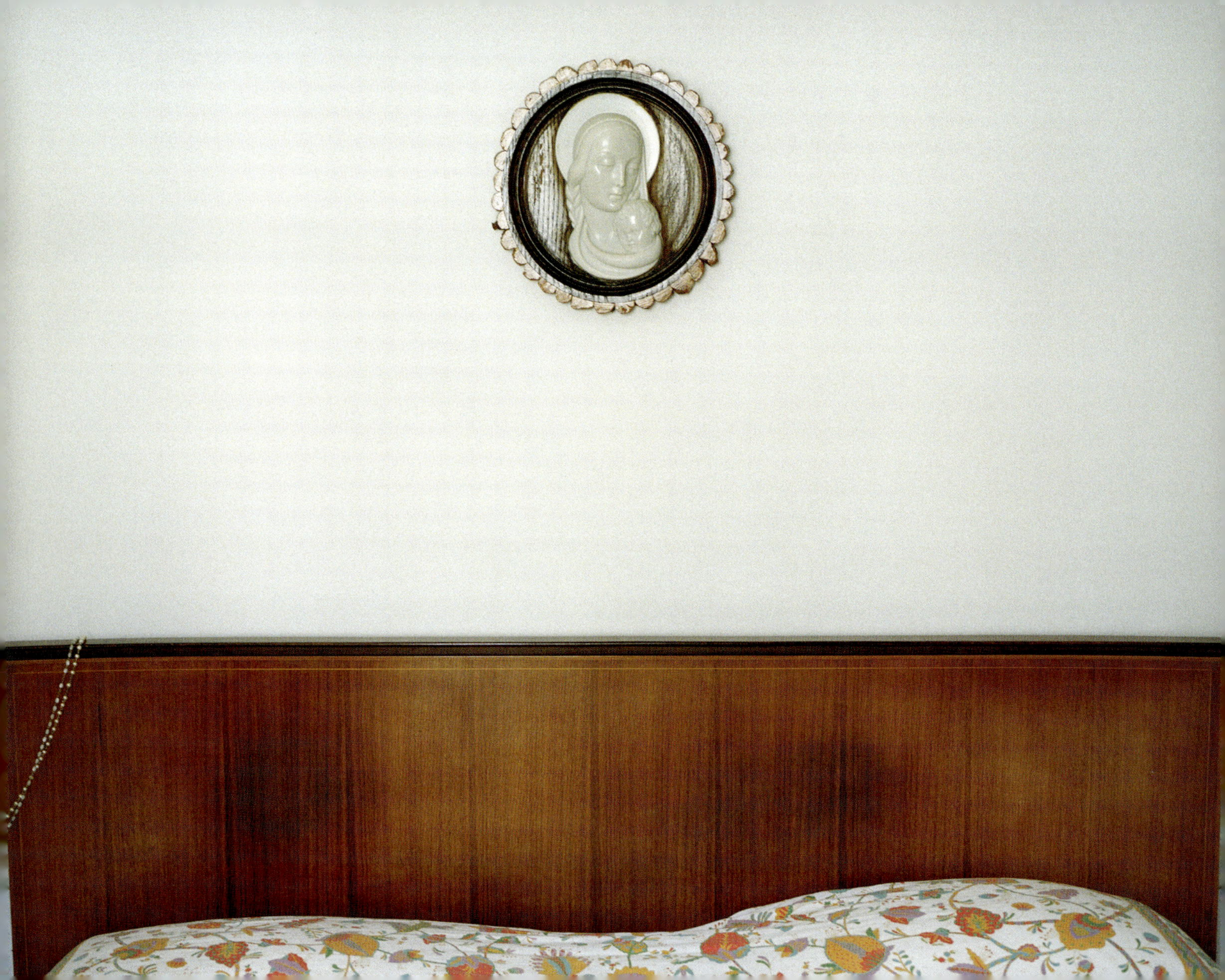

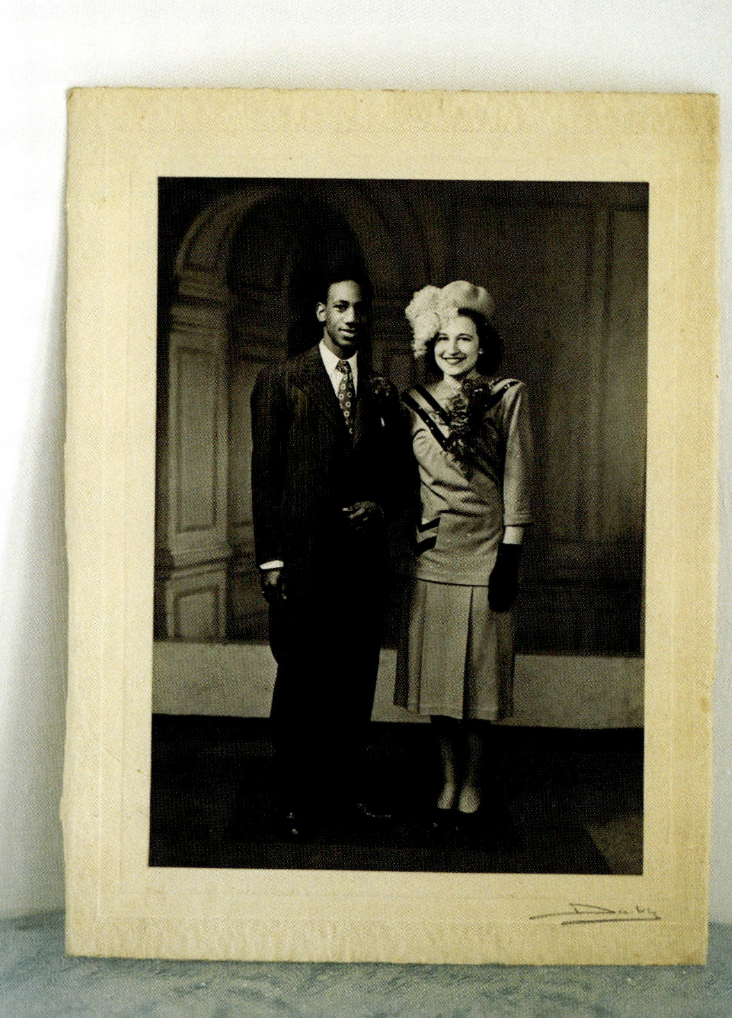

## Albert "Jake" and Mary Jacobs

Solihull, England

Married on April 27, 1948



*Mary* Jake said to me, "Would it ever be possible for me to marry you?" And I said, "Possible but not probable!" And that's how it was. It wasn't likely that I would ever marry him, and he knew that. So when he went home to Trinidad, my mother and father breathed a sigh of relief. But he used to write, and he said, "I'm thinking I might come back to England."

When he did come back, I met him at the local train station. Jake came off the train in a bright green suit that went in at the ankles. Oh, I was astonished! I stepped back and thought, what is this? What have I done? He wasn't in his military uniform anymore, so he didn't look like everybody else. But I was as helpful as I could be, and I told him I didn't think he would be able to get work in the North because they were short of work, especially now that the war had stopped. They weren't making ammunitions anymore, so they weren't employing people.

Jake decided to move to Birmingham, and again, my parents thought that was it. He was settling in Birmingham, and hopefully, he was going to get a job but he didn't get one. And there were many, many weeks before he got one. So my father, feeling very guilty about the fact that he'd come back to England, said, "Well, I better send the boy money." So he sent him money, and he paid his expenses until he got a job.

I was very fond of Jake, and we tried to think of ways that we could be together. One of the ways was that I had always wanted to teach, and because of the war I had taken up shorthand and typewriting so that I had something to fall back on. And I did use that for a short time, and I decided that I could use that again if I got a job in the Midlands. I could get a job and we could settle in the Midlands and we could get married but we had nowhere to stay. And nobody wanted to give us a room or rent us an apartment. No one wanted to be involved. So my father said, "If you go, you go and you don't come back and I don't want to ever see you again." I was crying, my mother was crying, it was very sad. I was very sorry that all this was going on in the air about him, you see. They were saying he was this, that and the other, and

I said he's not. He's just ordinary. He's just an ordinary boy. He just has a black face.

*Jake* There was one special area where most of the black people lived, which was rooms only. In those days, I don't think any black individual had a house. But if you go to these places—room to let by a white person—Mary would get a yes. But as soon as you say my husband is black, that's it. It's a different kettle of fish today. But I don't think a lot of people realized what black people had to put up with in those days.



*Mary* We were married in 1948 and I was just coming to the end of my teacher training and we desperately wanted somewhere to live. I came into Birmingham, and I met a lovely girl, Zena, and she had just got married the same time. She said, "Well, we decided some weeks ago to buy a house. It would be very small, but we wouldn't want to use the whole house because there's only the two of us at the moment. So if we could find another couple who would live upstairs, we would be very pleased." So I said, "You wouldn't have us would you?" And she said, "Can I think about it?" She wanted to talk to her parents. So I left it with her. In the meantime, I had one period and then I became pregnant and so I was having a baby.

I was crying all the time because I wanted to be with my mother, and my father wouldn't let me go and see her, wouldn't let me stay with them. Eventually, when I had got married and I was pregnant, he said that I could come and see mother. So I came home once on my own and saw my mother and my father sort of grunted. He really didn't say anything to me. And I asked if I could come again and if I could bring Jake with me and he said yes. So by this time we were married and I was pregnant and we got the top half of Zena's house and we were living there.

I wasn't very well carrying this baby. A friend of Jake's was a doctor, and he used to see me every month. And he just said, "Oh, you're getting better every week. You look marvelous." Of course the baby was growing, I hoped. And one day I went shopping and I had a fainting turn in the shop and I had to lie down. And they had to get someone to come and take me home. Eventually I…well, in a lot of strife and turmoil, I had the baby and it was born dead. It had already died when I had the fainting—the doctor said it must have happened. I didn't know what to do. I was very, very young, inexperienced. I had no support. Eventually, I went back to work, everything settled down. Zena moved on because her husband had got a promotion, and so they moved to another town.

*Jake* One Sunday morning she said, "We're gonna have a chat." We came downstairs and she said, "Look. We are moving out of the area. You sign here. The house is yours."

*Mary* So we took it over.

*Jake* And we have been very good friends for many years. We are still friends today. They don't class us as friends—they class us as family.

*Mary* In my life, I've tried to be upstanding. I've tried to be truthful and honest and good and everything that you should be. I've tried to be successful in my career. I've tried to be honest with the girls when I've talked to them and when I've advised them. I've tried to give them the right advice. And I feel that I've had a successful life in that respect. I've not had a family so I've missed out on that but other things have come up and I've had the pleasure of other people's children by teaching them. Being with them all the time. All that has made up for everything. I can't tell you how much I loved it and how happy I was. Not always with the marriage but with my circumstances, with what I've done with it. And there's nothing wrong with the marriage, but other people made it wrong. Other people looked in surprise.

*Jake* And I'm here to prove that they were wrong and I'm right. Love is all you know. Perhaps if you had something else to compare it with then you can say this is the difference. But as far as I'm concerned, there's no difference because I've always been on this side of it. I don't know if I hadn't had this what I would have.

*Mary* I feel successful in what I've done. And I don't mean that everybody should marry or have mixed marriages. I mean I have made the most of what I've got. I've let them see that it can work. It can happen. It isn't always a bad thing. It can be a good thing.

I think that I've made a mixed marriage that could have all the difficulties in the world less difficult and more ordinary. I just think that if you do something like that, be successful. Make the sacrifices worthwhile, and that's what I have done. In that way I'm happy. I've always been upstanding and always kept my dignity.



We're just normal—we quarrel, we fight, we talk to each other and try to reason things out—and I think everybody will say, even after 60 years, "There you are. We told you not to do it."

And I don't want them to say that. I want it to be said that it did happen and that it did turn out all right and that it's happening again in other parts of the world. Other people are doing the same thing. I wish them good luck. If they have something that I didn't have or I have something that they didn't have, I wish them good luck.

*Jake* What I would say is this—in order to have a successful marriage, the man has to be very tolerant. He has to hear and don't hear if you understand what I mean. And he has to be very versatile, always willing to say sorry. Or I didn't hear or I did not know. It's something that you have to work very

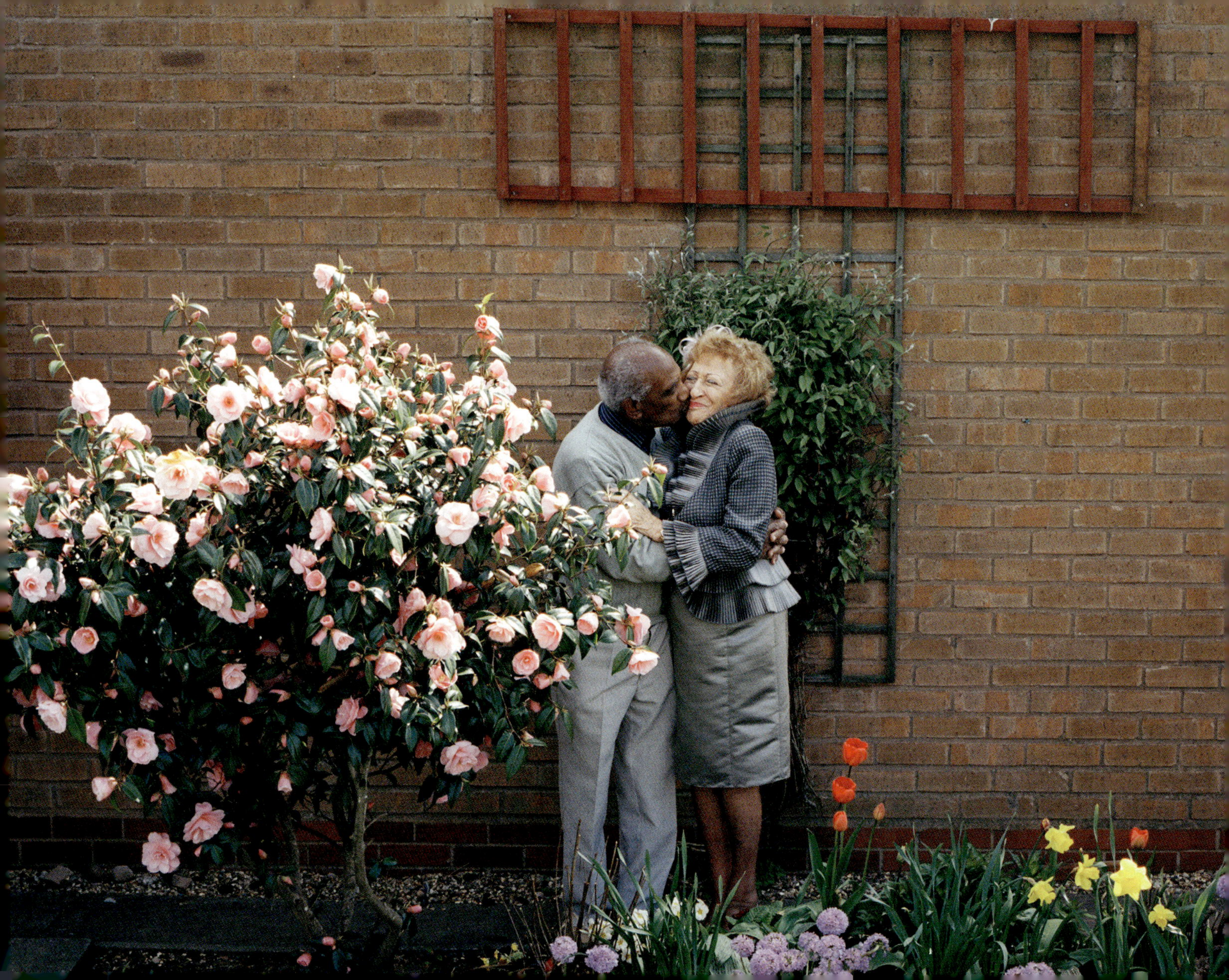

hard at without a doubt. And that would make a happy married life. You have to give, give and give.

*Mary* No matter who you're married to you have quarrels. It's the up and down thing. And you have to work at it. Everybody has to work at it. And I never like to be beaten by anything. I like to think that I can overcome anything. When I go somewhere now and people see me and then suddenly Jake joins me and they look, you can tell by the way they look at you whether they approve or disapprove.

*Jake* Hang on. You've got a husband who brings you a cup of tea every morning. You've got a husband who does all the cooking for you. You've got a husband who does all the cleaning.

*Mary* He's very good. He helps me. But sometimes he just doesn't think. He's like any other man—he just doesn't think.

*Jake* Or is it you who just doesn't think?

*Mary* I know. I know. It's six of one and half a dozen of the other. But that's it really. It's overcoming difficulties, and I'm not unhappy with anything I've done. I did all the things I've wanted to do and that's it. I'd like to have won a million on the lottery but never mind.

*Jake* I told Mary if we ever win a million, the following day she would drop dead.

*Mary* Thank you.

*Jake* You know why? You worry too much. That's going to be your problem, love. I know that. You're going to be worried too much. We've got plenty. We're all right. If we were to win that sort of money, we'd give it away without a doubt. We would give it away. Am I right?



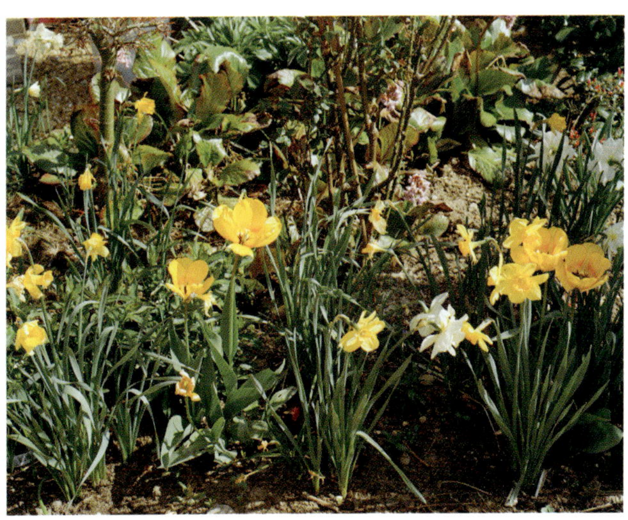

## Itig and Golda Pollac

Brooklyn, New York
Married on August 13, 1946



*Golda* We knew each other before the war, but we never spoke. He was with other girls because he was much, much older than me. You know, he was very nice-looking! He was a tailor, and he had a place where he made suits for men. When we came back from the war, he had gone to my sister's house. I was staying with her. In August of this year, we will have been married 63 years. I would say love came little by little. Not right away. We were young. And he was older, but I liked him. He spoke to me in a very nice way.

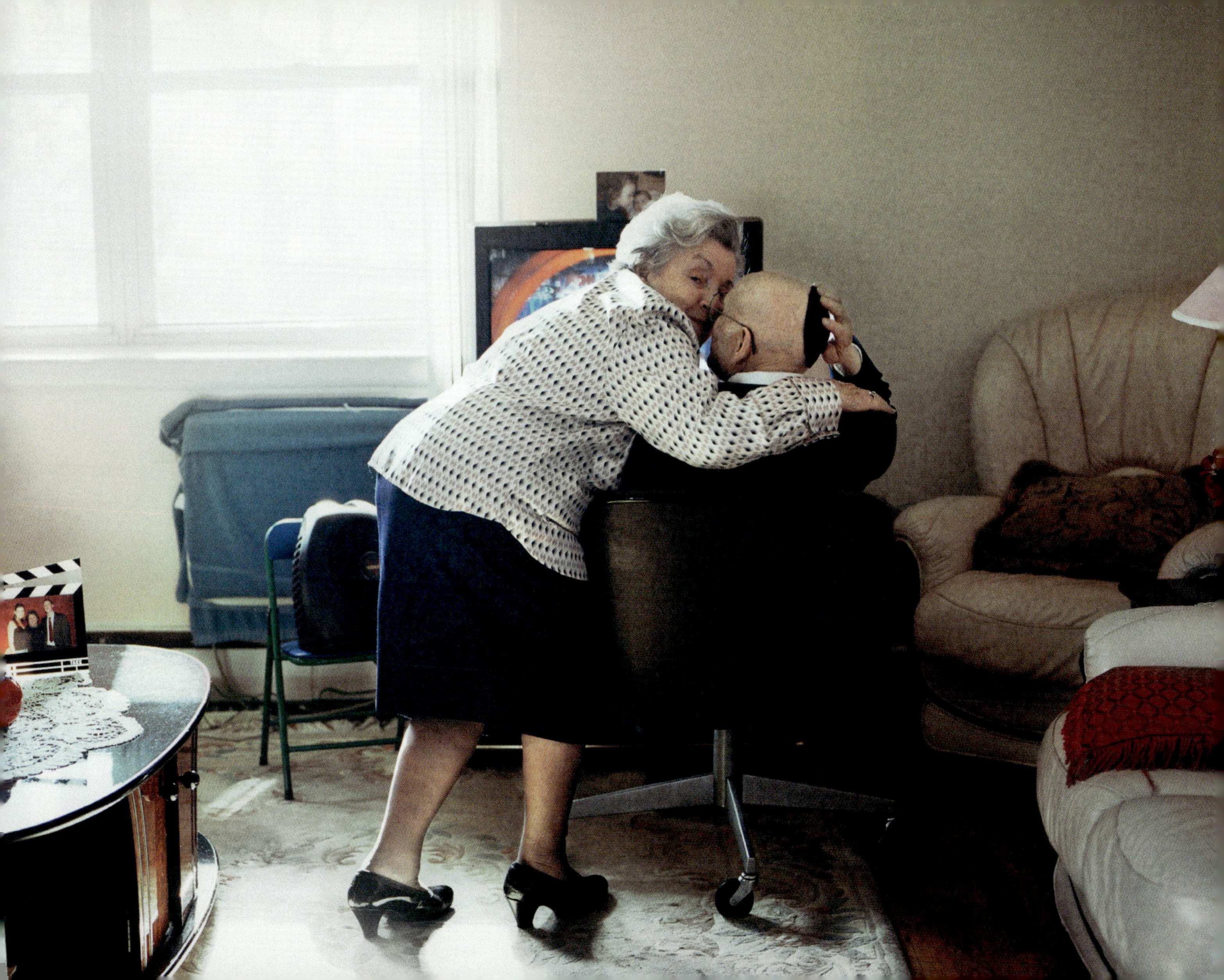

## Gino and Angie Terranova

Staten Island, New York

Married on September 27, 1947



*Angie* You really don't think about getting older. First of all, you're aging together, and when you see a person constantly, you don't notice big changes. Like you don't notice, oh you're getting a little wrinkle here and tomorrow you say it's a little deeper. No, those are things that just happen. You don't pay attention to those things. I mean, I'm not thinking every day, "Oh my husband's 83 years old, he's gonna be 84, oh my goodness, I'm married to an old man!" And I hope he feels that way too.

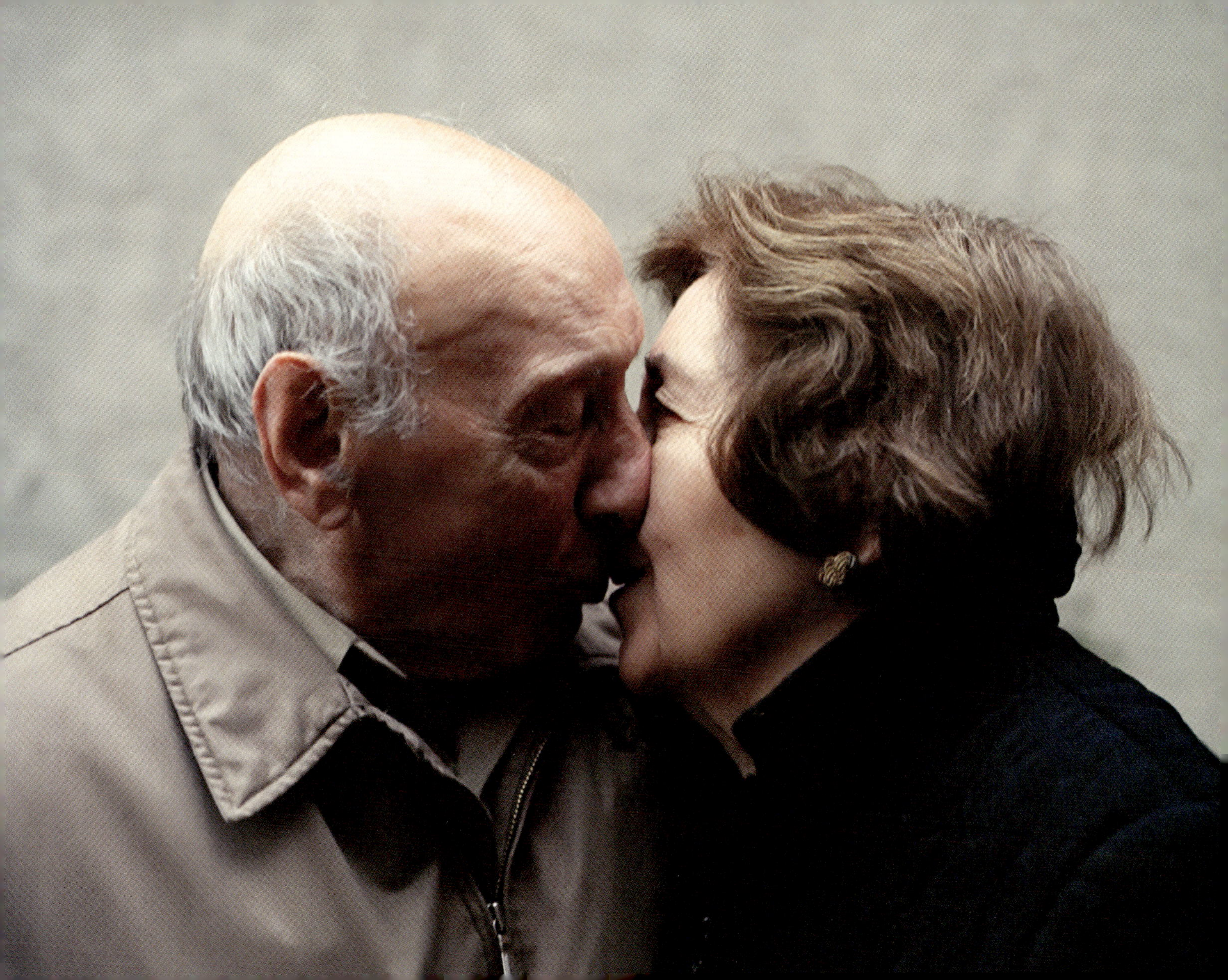

## Jack and Cynthia Octigan

Boise, Idaho
Married on February 19, 1950



*Cynthia* We met in Los Angeles in 1949. I was there working in an office, and the lady that owned the office was a patient of my father's. My father was a doctor at the Mayo Clinic, and she wanted to do something nice for my father, so she hired me. And shortly after I was there, I met Jack Octigan. The way we met in that great big city was that he was looking for a wife. He was 25, and he talked to his mother and said, "Mom, do you know any nice lady, anybody that has a niece or a daughter that's from a nice family?" And a couple weeks later she called back, and she said, "Jack, I have a phone number for you." It was my phone number, and he called me about five times before he could get a hold of me. We just had a great time when we first met. I think we had about three dates and decided that we wanted to be together forever.

I think the key to a good marriage is having a good family relationship before you ever get married, and that's what we had. We had everything in common, and we just had a wonderful time together. I'm thankful for every day I get. We know that it's coming to an end, but that's OK, we know where we're going. Jack's 89 and I'm 84, and we feel very fortunate that we've had each other this long because many people don't. But we'll take what comes and be very thankful for the years we've had. I couldn't ask for anything more, and I think the Lord would be pleased with us. That's what we want to do, we want to please the Lord.

I think young people today don't really look for the right things in a mate. They're so physically attracted to each other that they think that's right. There's a lot more to it than that. You have to have the same upbringing, and you have to have the same likes. We've always been involved in Christian work, we've always gone to church. It's just the way we live. I think if you don't have that kind of background, a lot of couples make it, but they have a lot of trouble in between. So I think faith is very important, it's very important in our family.

*Jack* It's great when every day is a new day of heaven. We've never had an argument, and we've always been communicative. She's done a fine job of giving a resume, and I'll tell you I couldn't have done it.

*Cynthia* Well, he could have years ago but he can't now. Jack really has good health aside from his memory. That's OK. We have a good time anyway. You have to accept what you're given. Most people who are 89 have something wrong with them and we're thankful and we just make do with what we have and try to serve where we can serve.

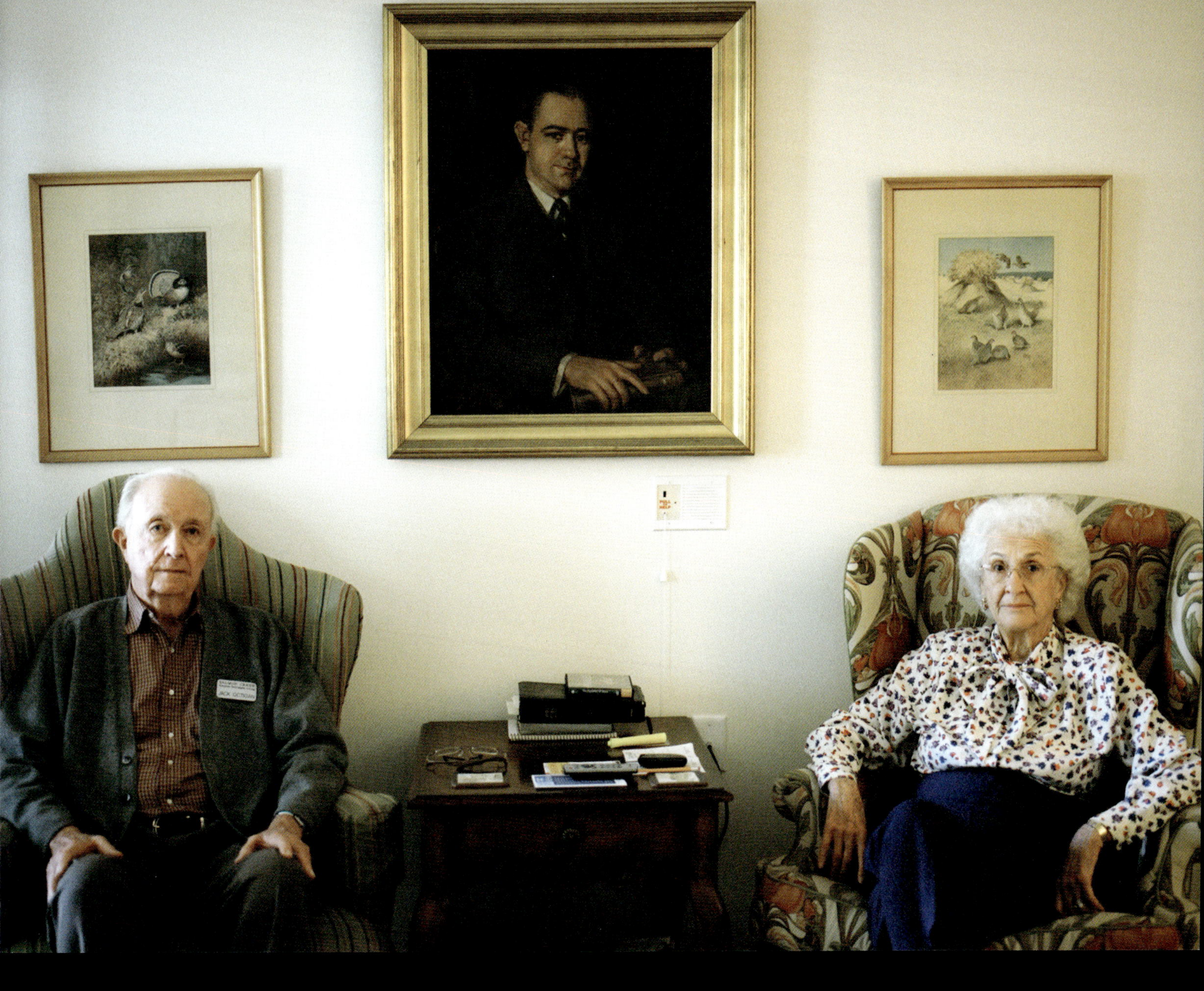

**Matts and Britta Mattson**

Vaxholm, Sweden

Married on May 15, 1959

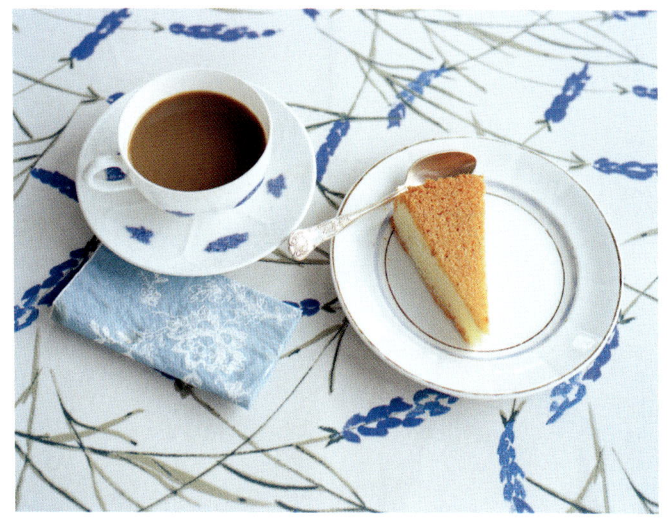

*Britta* Matts was not my first love. I had a couple of years meeting a man who stayed in Uppsala, so we were taking the train up and down and saw a lot of each other. The first man didn't want me to educate myself. He wanted me to be at home. Then when I left him, he regretted that and tried to get me back, but I didn't want to.

When Matts and I fell in love, it was like when he touched me I was happy. That was the beginning, and then it matured to other feelings. With time there was more of an attraction. A sense of safety and happiness together. I feel that I am safe in the neighborhood of my husband. And I think he is honest too. In love, we see the one we want to see, and they are safe.

When you think back, you realize that from the birth to when I met my husband was a whole life. And when you look back, it seems like a very big period before we married, but that becomes less and less compared with what we have now. We have so much—so many experiences now than those years before.

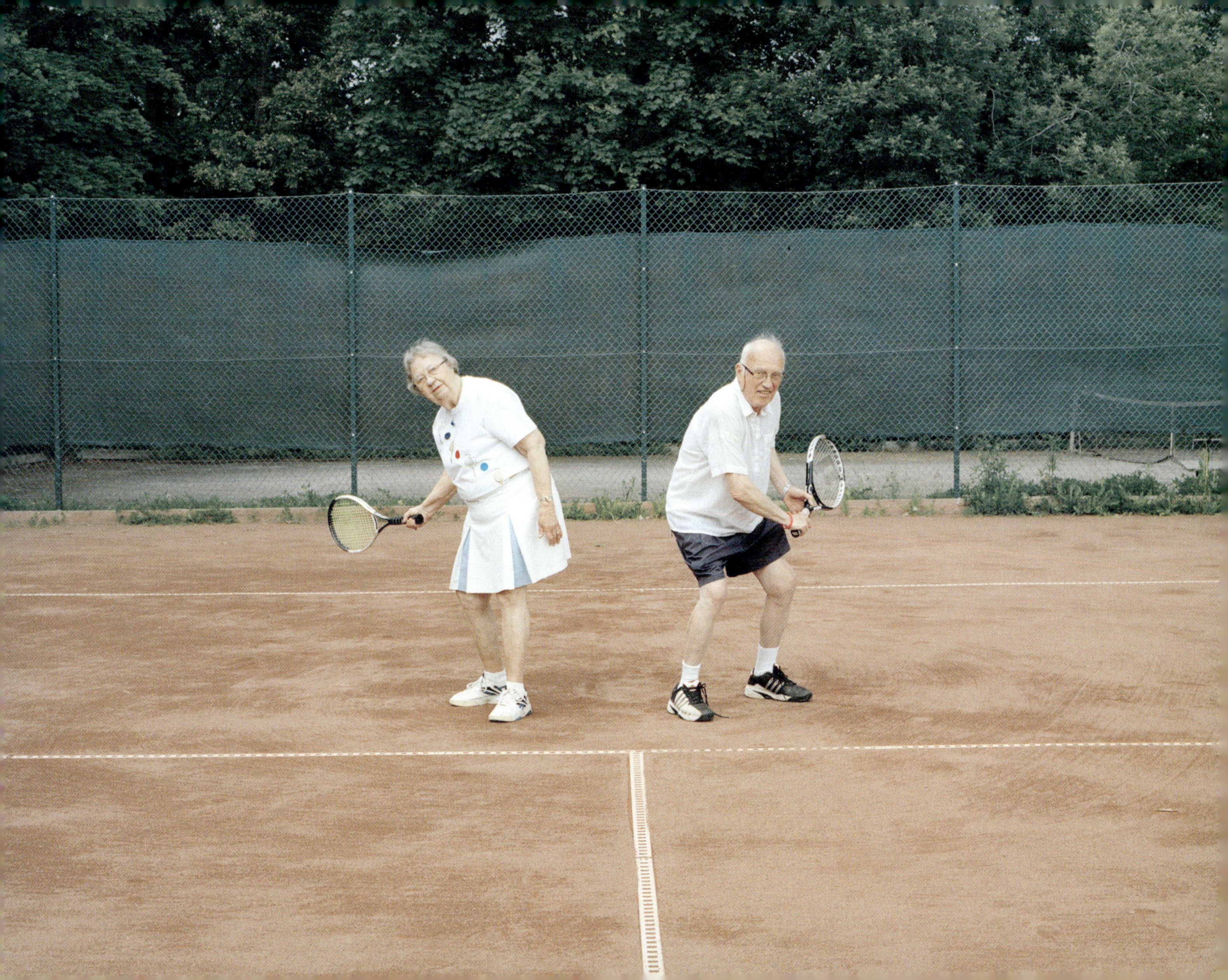

## Woolf and Hélène Marmot

Le Vésinet, France
Married on May 8, 1947



*Woolf* Greater efforts have to be made to adjust to someone whose every single thing, every single reaction is different from those you're brought up with. Those extra difficulties either make for a stronger marriage or a weaker one, which will break in those circumstances.

I will tell you a little story. The daughter of one of my best friends got married in London. We were invited and somebody got up to make a speech, and he said, "You must not forget every morning when you get up, you must tell your wife that you love her." And I felt like being sick when I heard it. Because this is exactly the kind of, I don't know exactly how to put...exactly the way you must not live because this is a duty. The same thing is Americans will say "Good-bye, love you!" It makes me ill because love is much more deep, solid, inexpressible. It's something which you feel and which you show in so many different ways. And speech is not the important thing. And I do really believe that. Our daughter, who lives 800 meters away, comes to see us most days. She certainly phones one, two, three, four times. I don't remember the last time I told her I love her but I do. I don't remember the last time I told my wife I love her. I show it to her 20 times a day. Little attentions. Caring. Like remembering to say when I'm going out. I just don't suddenly disappear. It's little things that matter in life. Not big things. And certainly not declarations.

*Hélène* Love is capital. It's basic. I couldn't imagine living without him. Absolutely. It was sensible, it was practical, it was wonderful. We were very different, and we obviously had to make efforts not to shock the other too much or the other's family too much. We avoid hurting the other with the wrong word, with the wrong gesture. We make efforts. We are different, so it always means efforts to come closer to what the other one might hope for. We made it, we did it.

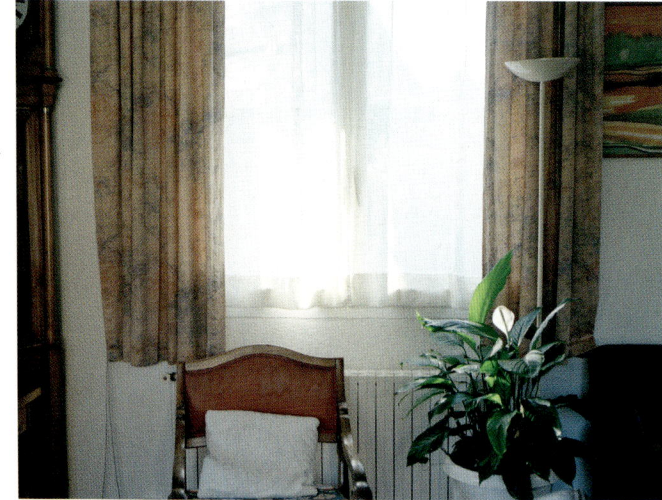

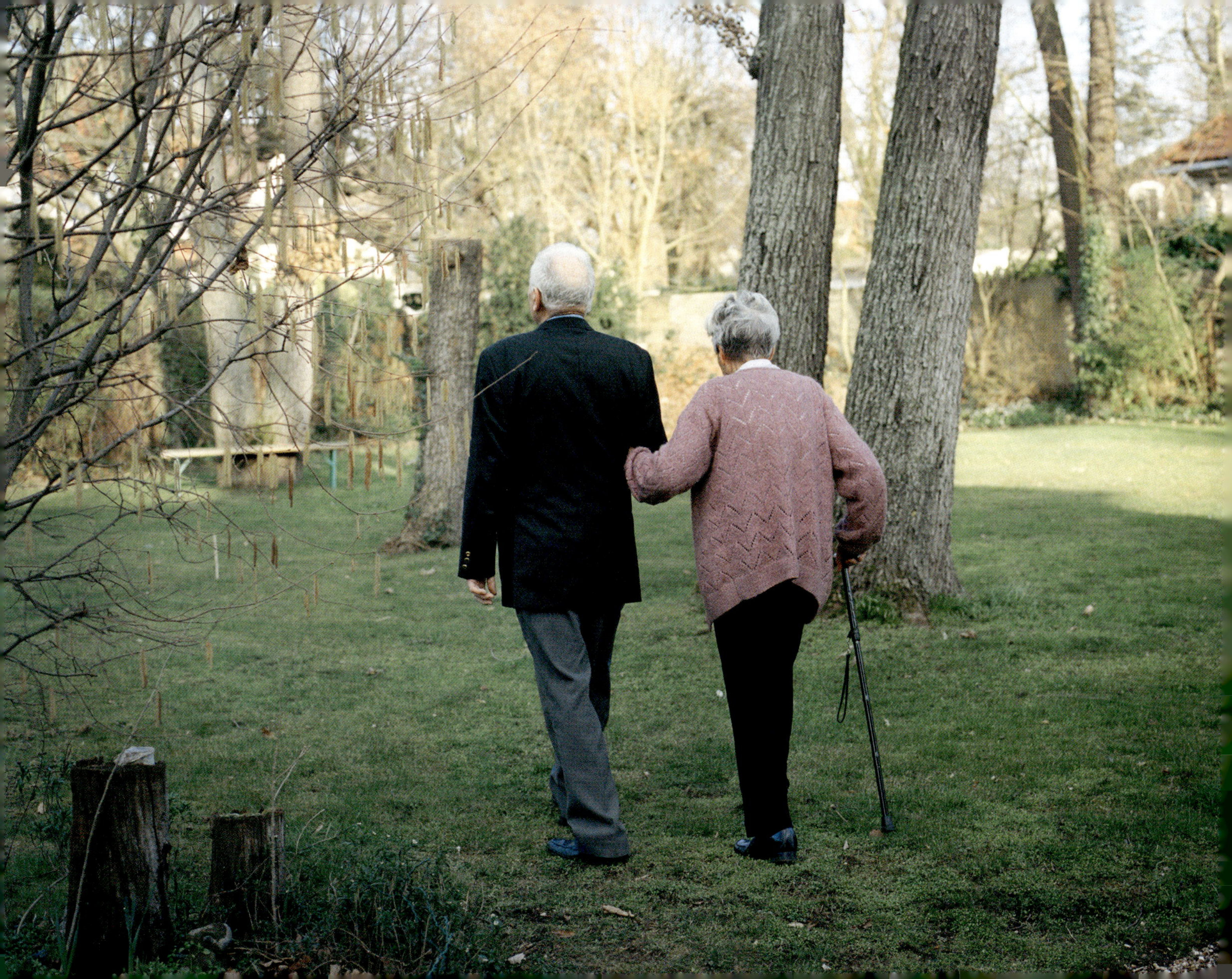

## Karam and Kartari Chand

Bradford, England

Married on December 11, 1925



*Karam* My trick is to make Kartari laugh. I like to tell jokes and make her smile. Being funny is my way of being romantic. I have been told laughing makes you live longer–my wife is still alive, so it must have worked. I love her, and I want to spend another 80 years by her side.

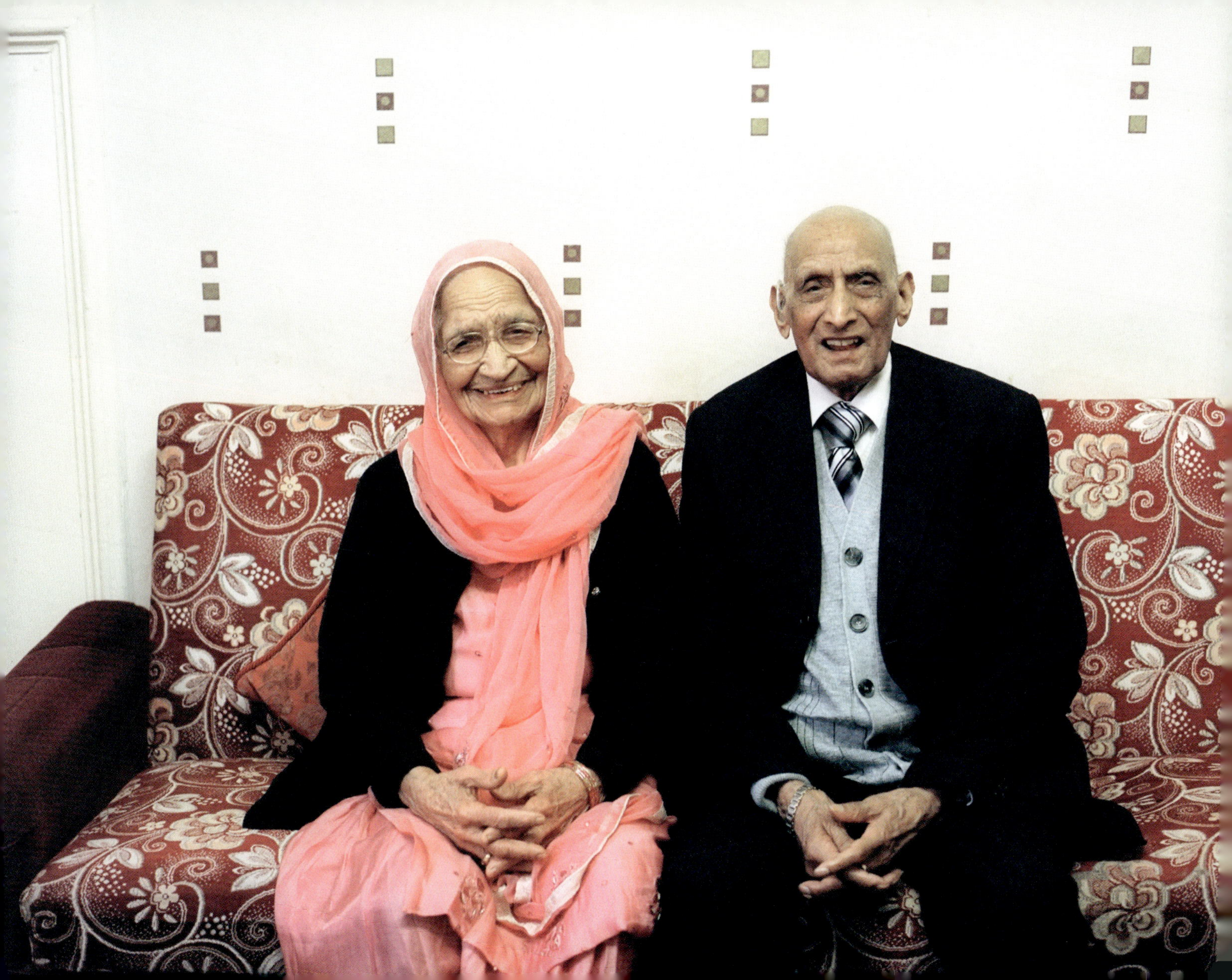

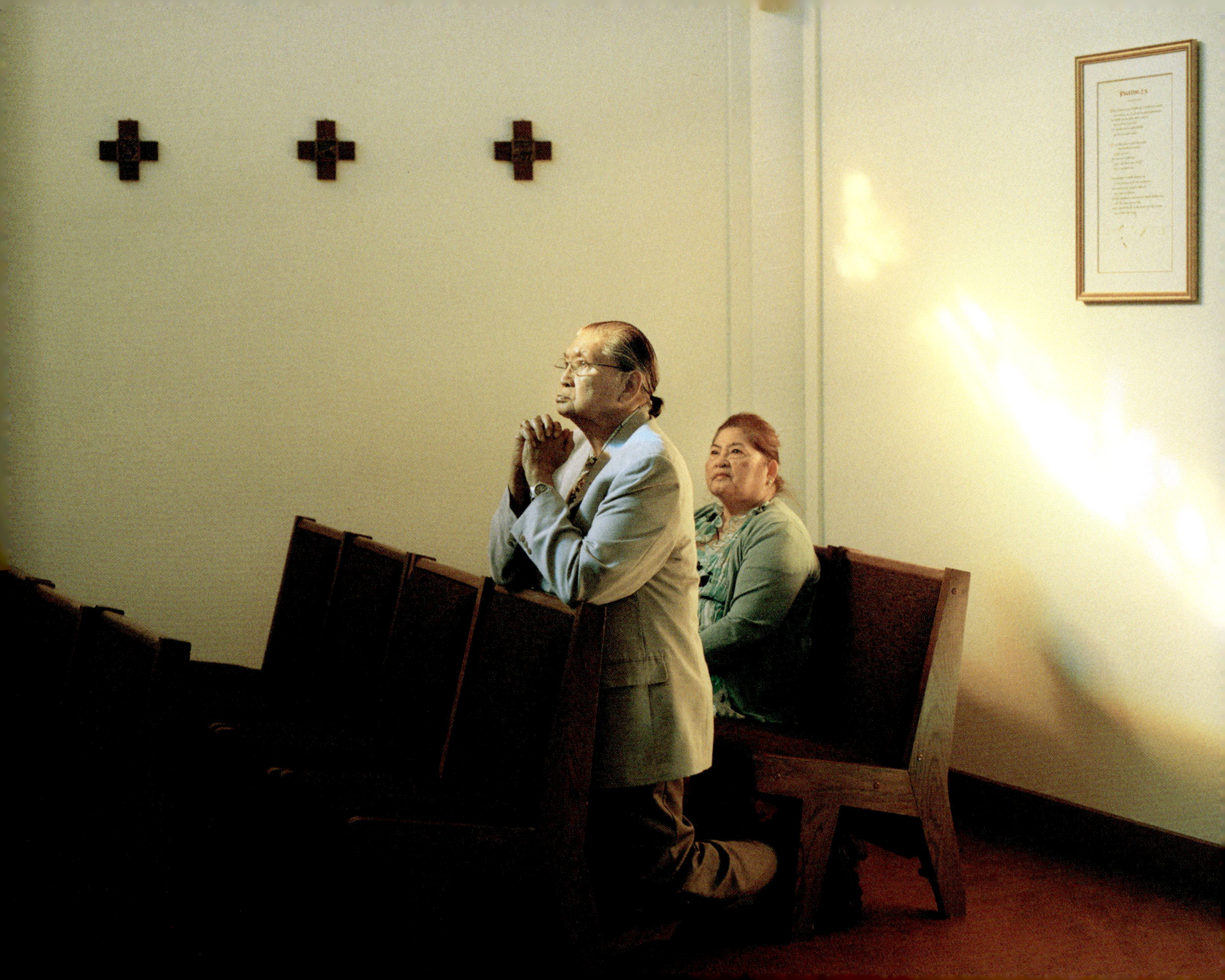
Psalm 23

## **Rodolfo and Vilma Gaspar**

Dublin, California

Married on October 15, 1959

*Vilma* We married 54 years ago in Manila. I used to be a Legion of Mary. I wanted to be a nun. I spent almost two years preparing, but unfortunately, I got sick. I had gastroenteritis and they brought me to the hospital and they decided that I could not carry on the duty of a missionary.

*Rodolfo* She became employed where I was already working as a teller. And that's where we met and I courted her.

*Vilma* He was so persistent! My friends were telling me, "Don't be angry with him because one of these days you're going to swallow your words." I was praying hard, and I had so many suitors. Most of the time I said, "I'm sorry, I don't love you. You have to stop coming and visiting me." But in his case, it was different. The first time he kissed me it was on the forehead. And that, for Filipinos, is a sign of respect.

*Rodolfo* For our wedding, we were having our car decorated with flowers, and it's supposed to be done only on the outside. But then on the day I was getting my car, there was a previous wedding that was supposed to be early in the morning, but the couple did not arrive. They cancelled out. So all the flowers that were supposed to be placed on their car were also placed inside of our car. Our car was full of flowers.

*Vilma* On the first night I talked to him and laid down the rules. If we were to be married and we have a problem, in order to stay together, we have to settle it before the night is over. Even if we're quarreling, we can settle it right away. I just said to him that this is what I want to be able to live happily. He's a man, he's a rascal, and he does so many things that I as a woman don't like, so I tell him right then and there. I don't keep anything inside because it hurts.



*Rodolfo* In the nature of my work, I used to visit branches of the bank, and the managers wanted to get approval for what they were doing. So they would take me out. We would go dancing to the night clubs, and sometimes I wouldn't get back to Manila until one o'clock in the morning.

*Vilma* I know he's been gallivanting all his years, all his life. And so I am prepared, and I said, "If you do that, then that is the end of our relationship."

*Rodolfo* No, but it is the fault of those girls. They were running after me. In my position it was very likely that there will be some girls that are interested in you. Sometimes they are the daughter of some rich businessman who wanted to get approval from the bank, so they throw you a party and introduce you to that lady. But that's it. I do not want to destroy my family with girls. I keep my faith.

## Lazar and Anna Galak

Brooklyn, New York
Married on February 20, 1952



*Anna* I don't try to understand the secret to love. You have to think not only about yourself. We sometimes had confrontations, but they were small. He worked very hard, and he was often tired.

I don't think mostly the point in love is the sex. It's absolutely not the main thing. It's the softness of the person that is with you, the friendship, the things that you say to each other. I love to sit near him. Everybody loves him, maybe more than me! He's a softer person. Until today, women like him very much. Really, but we are usually always together.

I send him to walk sometimes because it's good for his health, but I look at the clock, worrying about why he is taking so long. It's the same for him. He calls me on my cell phone, "Where are you?" I say, "I only bought the tomatoes. I still need to buy apples!" Try to understand, this is how I explain love. But now love carries more of a responsibility because we are older, and we've had many medical problems. "Did you take the pills?" Every day, that's our life now. I think this is like a ray of love. I didn't forget you.

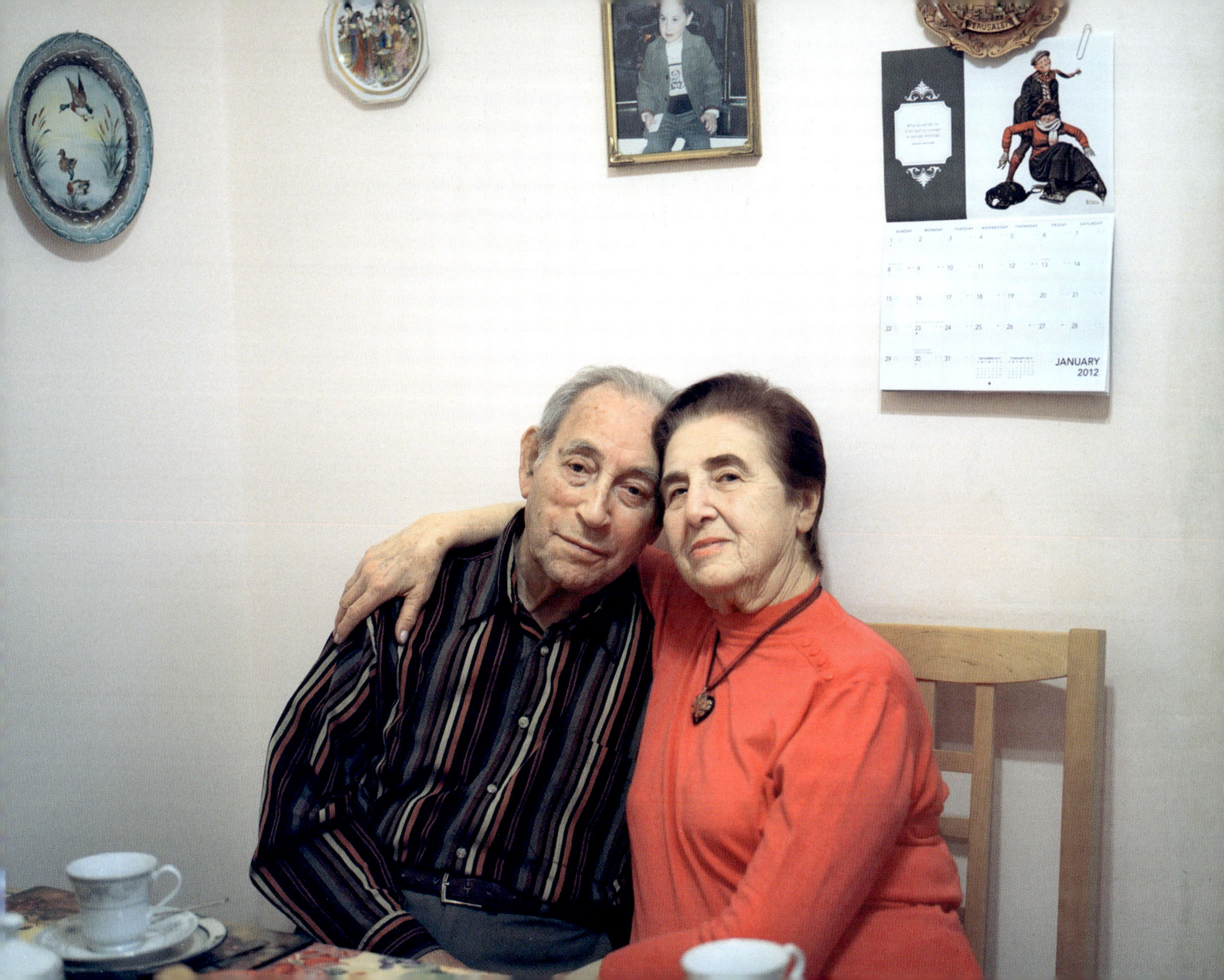
JANUARY
2012

## Eric and Elisabeth MacKay

Lenzie, Scotland

Married on August 28, 1956



*Elisabeth* I had heard about Eric from my roommate, who thought he was a bit special. And when they said, "Hello, Eric," I realized that it was this Eric, and I knew that if there was ever to be anybody, it was to be him. But it was so definite that I really had to ask God to look after it because we were both Christians, and I thought, well if this is right, Father, please look after it. I didn't know him then, but I just knew that he was the right person. I am a bit like that. I do have sort of instincts about things sometimes, especially when it's very important.

We used to go early to the Christian Union prayer meetings. I used to run down from the residence and I was quite sure on my feet in those days and I would hear the beat coming behind me and pretend not to notice and be very surprised when he caught up with me. Gradually, it came to both of us that we were very much in love. I think it wasn't very long after I first met him really. I don't know how long it took Eric to realize, but I think I realized it a bit more quickly.

When I first went to his parents' house, after we knew that we had an understanding, his mother was very warm and welcoming and his father was very polite, but there was a certain ice that I could sense. So when he was on his own a little bit later in the sitting room, I said, "Well, what's wrong?" Which took him a little bit aback. And he said, "Well, it's not your fault—it's just that you're English and I am afraid that Eric will join the Church of England and leave the Church of Scotland." So we had a long talk, and after that we were the best of friends.

I think it's important to tell each other exactly how you feel and not bottle it. Things get resentful and that's bad. It's much better to talk and say what you feel. My husband is very kind, and he's a very good cook. When I'm ill, he takes over completely, so I don't have to worry about feeding him when I'm ill. And he's very courteous. Sometimes he makes me cross but not very often.

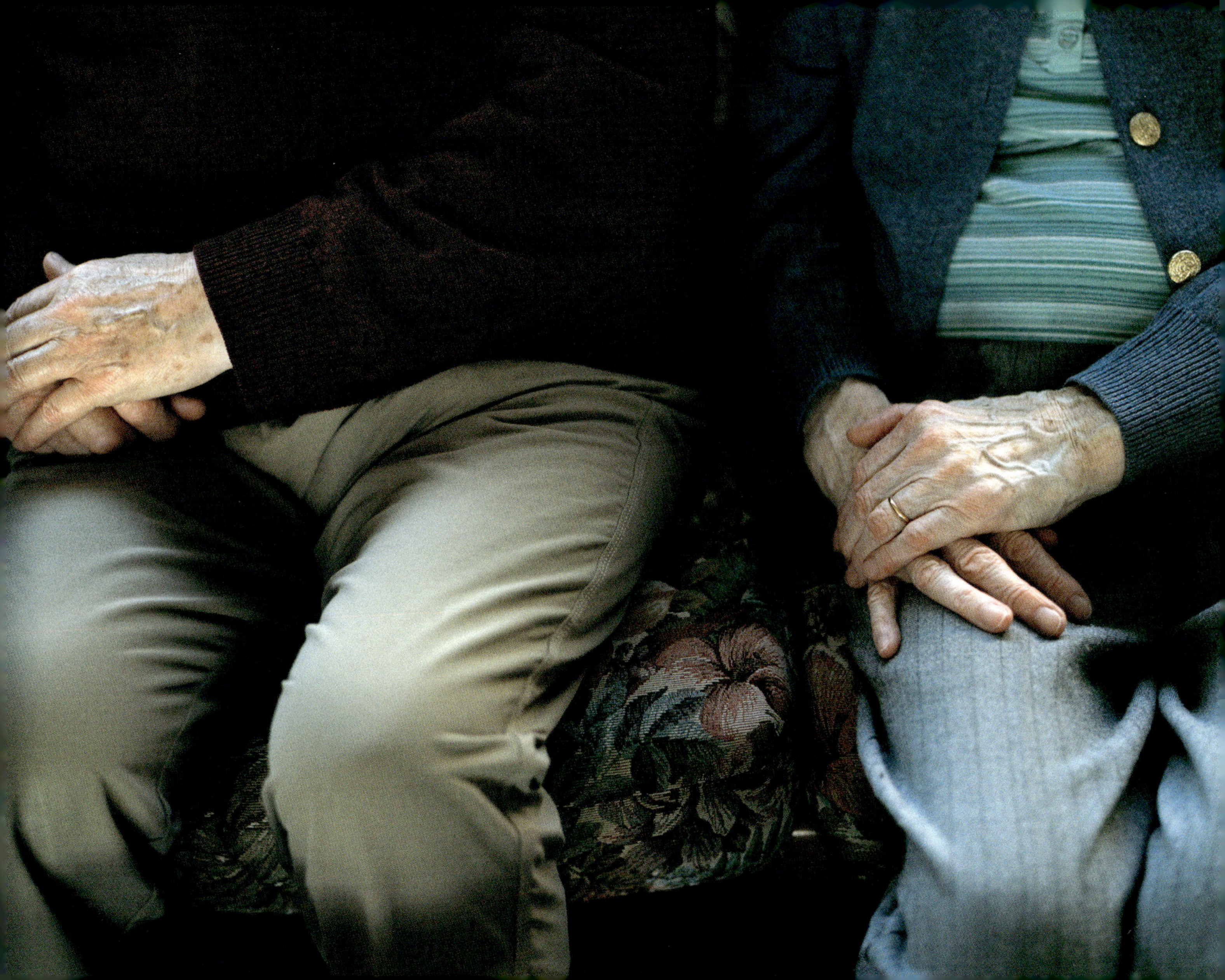

*Eric* My fate was sealed, I had no idea. We then had to face the parents because my father had fairly strong feelings about church, and he was afraid that with Elisabeth being a strong character she might alter my views.

She says that I am too courteous. If she's dealing with a tradesman who's not very good, she says I'm far too polite. And she's been quite ill, she broke her shoulder and that was very serious and lasted a long time. We've had to care for each other completely at times, and it's not made us further apart. In a way one imagines that one retains the same abilities as one always had. I've always run and this last year is the only time that I've not been able to run and that is slightly annoying. It slows one up. One has to be content with doing less. Elisabeth's not so happy driving long distances, and I've had to do more of the long-distance driving. We've got a caravan and we still enjoy that but we have cut down some of the things that we did but we keep in contact with people. We don't tend to entertain as much as we used to, and we probably don't go out to eat as much but we are happy to sit at home.

I think we know each other's thoughts. We'll come up with the same idea quite frequently. Or Elisabeth will say something, and I'll say, "Yes, I was wondering about that." So that's quite fun. We don't have to talk all the time.

We've had enough through our life. We've not been short. We haven't been very wealthy, but we've had enough. We've been able to give our children the education they wanted. Four of them are married, and we just pray that they have the same as we have.

## Alibey and Esma Kudar

Tahtakuşlar, Turkey
Married on September 5, 1954



*Esma* The love between us has never changed. Does love ever change?

*Alibey* There are no old loves anymore. Today's loves are spoiled very quickly. We never fought in 57 years, we could not.

*Esma* If you ask who spent their lives without a fight, that'd be us. Today times are very different. When we were married, I never had my own wedding dress. My husband had eight brothers and sisters, four of each, and me and his four sisters all were married in the same dress. Then, when his mother died, we buried her in the dress because it had been hers.

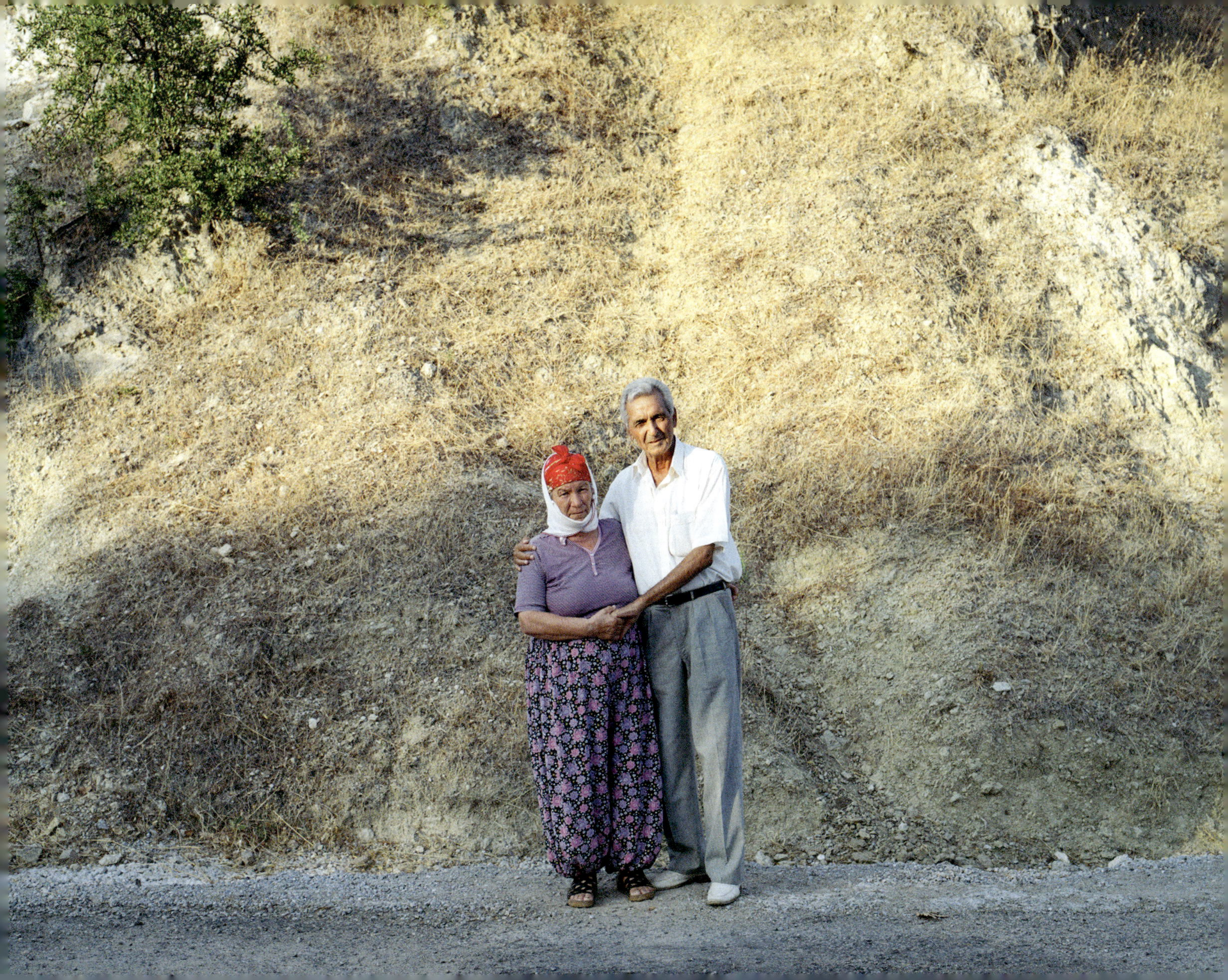

## Chong and Sung Kwak

Manalapan, New Jersey
Married on October 5, 1959



*Sung* My family had introduced me to my husband in Suwon, South Korea. I got a call from my relatives while I was at work saying that I needed to go to their home because there was a man they wanted me to meet. This was the way things were in terms of arranged marriages. We dated for about a year before we were married.

We had about 500 people at our wedding. Guests came from my workplace, my husband's workplace, and then we had all our friends and relatives. In our culture it's hard for you to turn down an invitation once you are invited. I was very happy, not because there were a lot of people, but because I felt I met the right person. Even after 50 years, we still don't have any big arguments. He always listened to me, and I always tried to do the right thing for him.

Back then in Korean society, when you turn 55, you had to leave the workplace. So I think we felt pressure. What are we going to do after my husband's retired? In Korea we didn't see a great many people having success after retirement. We had a chance to come to the United States, and so we decided that was the right thing to do for the family. To come to the United States and make a new beginning. We started a dry cleaning business here, and although I was physically tired because I was not used to working all day, I was pretty happy and had less stress. Here there were not many things to worry about. In the morning I would go to work, and the school would take care of the children. I didn't have any high expectations. I knew that I was not going to be a millionaire, but I was happy that I worked and made a good living.

My husband had a stroke last year, and now I am the one who really tries to help him. Before he got sick, he took care of all the gardening. I wanted to help him out, but he said, "No, I want to do it my own way." So he didn't let me do the gardening work with him, but now we really need to maintain the garden together.

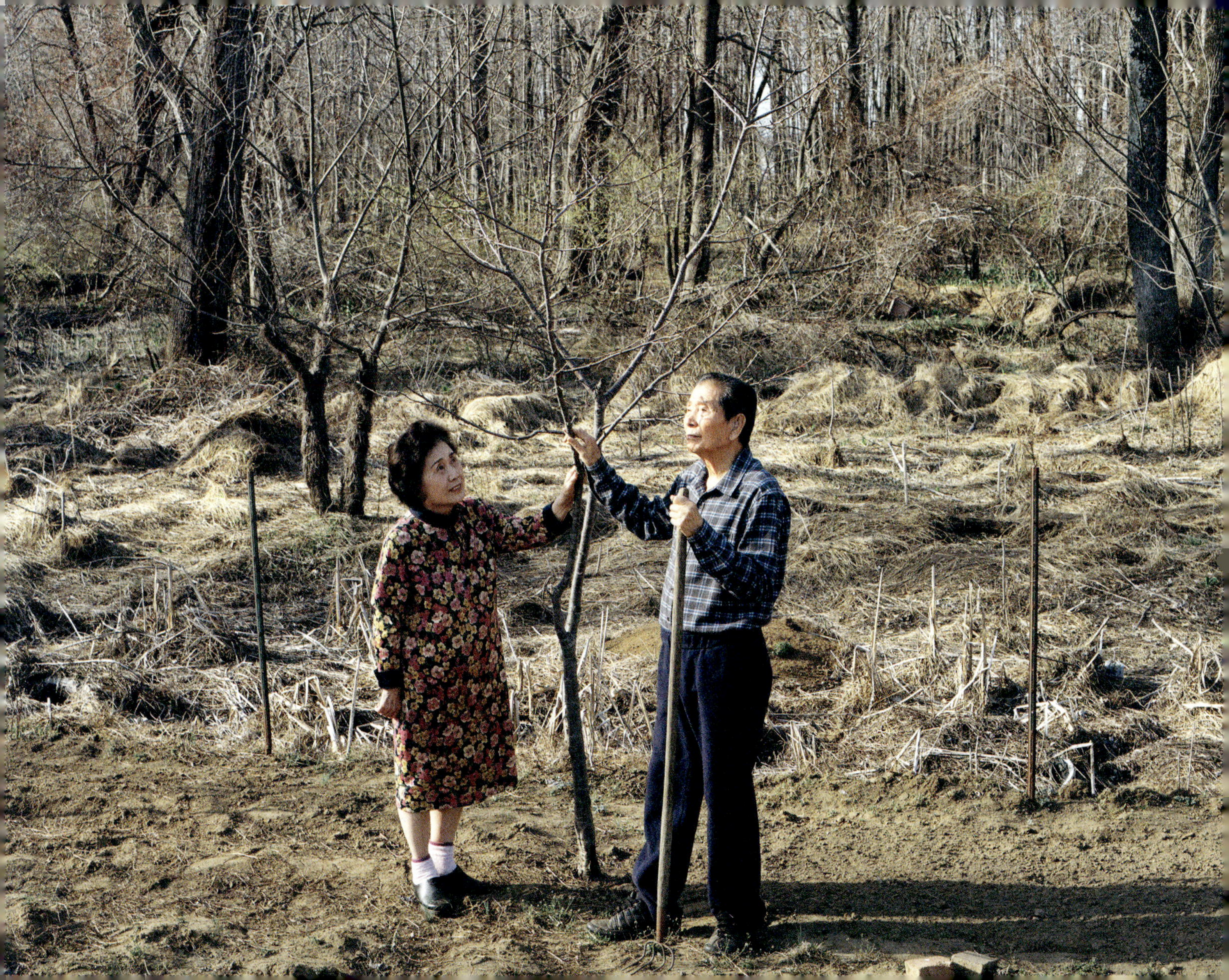

## Suresh and Anarkali Vijayakar

Tampa, Florida
Married on December 19, 1954



*Suresh* I studied in a boys' school and didn't have any real interaction with female students. One didn't have the word *girlfriend*. In those days we used to have arranged marriages—somebody from the community or family will think of some young girl somewhere and a young boy somewhere and say, "Ah, I think they will be a good match for each other." And then they will talk to the two families. So in our case a common friend thought that we should get together.

*Anarkali* He saw me walking on the bridge over the railway line, crossing to the other side where the meeting point was. And he was so nervous that he just walked away. And this lady who was supposed to introduce us, she said, "I don't know what has happened." So after a long time, he came wiping his wrists with a handkerchief, and the lady asked him, "Where have you been?" "Oh, I went to buy some kerchiefs for my mother."

*Suresh* I didn't know how to bluff.

*Anarkali* I was in a huff, I was angry because I was just 15, I was not even out of school. And that is why he saw me walking in a huff, and he said, "Oh, this is not going to work out." You know, I was not ready for this kind of thing. The thought of coming to know somebody and thinking of marriage. But when he went home that night he wrote a letter asking me if I would like to meet him again. And my father wrote the reply saying, "Yes, of course, we'll meet." So that is how he came to pick me up a couple of days later. He came and I walked down and he said, "You know, there's some powder on your cheek." And I said, "Oh my God, my mother!" Because she wanted me to look very fair. And he said, "What, your mother still puts powder on you?"

*Suresh* Within three months of us first meeting, I was offered a scholarship, and I had to go abroad. So that is when our parents thought we should get engaged. We had a ceremony that made the proposal official. So the two years that I was away gave her time to get to know our family and complete two more years of schooling.

*Anarkali* We have horoscopes made at birth. When the proposal goes from the girl's side to the boy's, they send the horoscope to see if the two horoscopes match. The idea is if they think that the girl is suitable for the boy, they keep that horoscope and send a huge cone of sugar in silver paper, which meant that we have accepted the proposal. That was the custom.

*Suresh* During this time there was never a question of are we compatible? Will we be able to make a good married

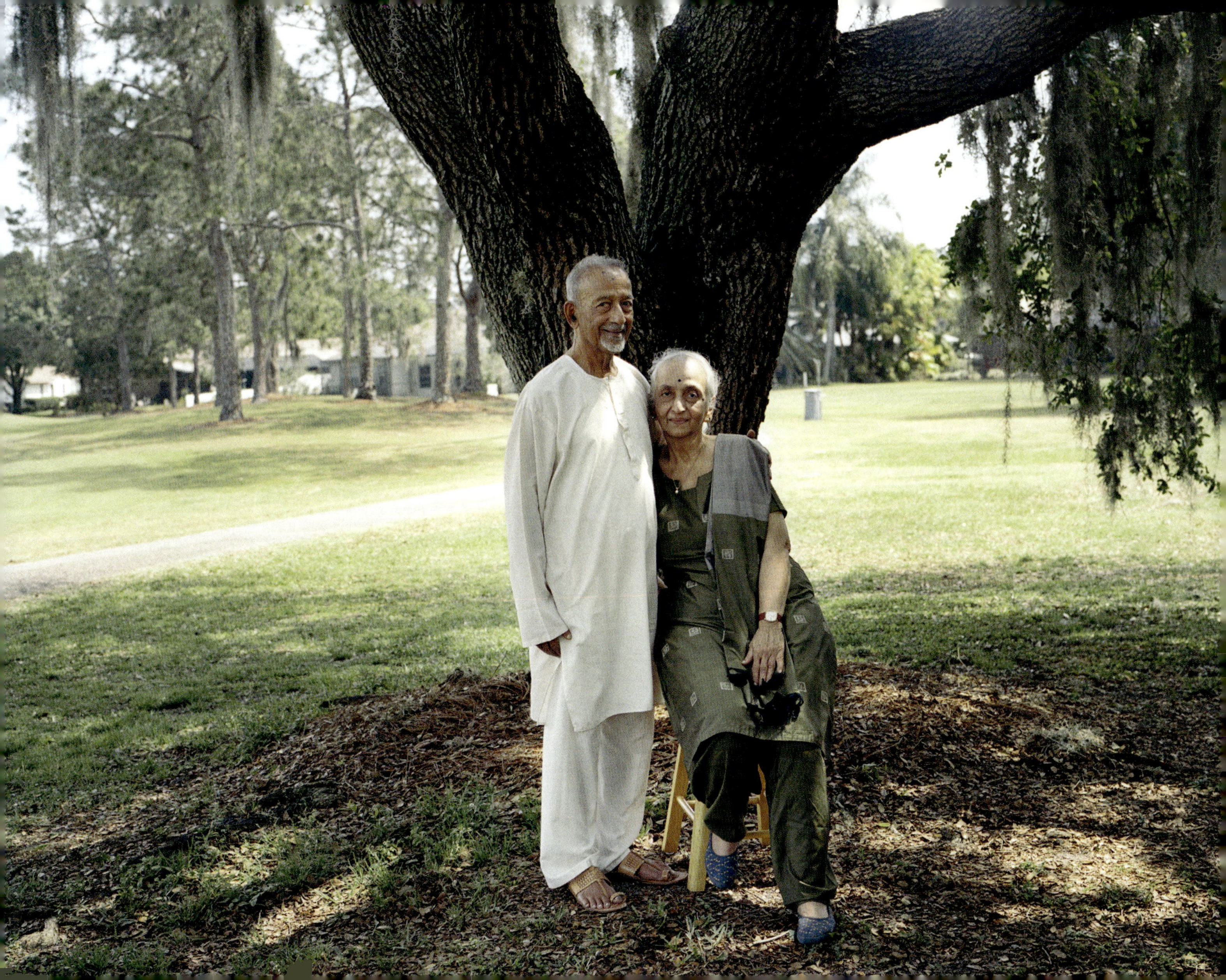

life? I mean, today there is so much discussion and debate. Our situation was totally different. Sex before marriage was unheard of in our days, our culture. In fact, how you plan your parenthood was not known. I remember having to somehow get hold of some books and was secretly trying to read.

*Anarkali* Once he said, "Do you think we'll be happy?" And I said, "Happiness is in the mind."



*Suresh* That time I remember I was thinking of what type of job I'll get, how much salary I would earn. So I asked her, "Do you think we'll be able to manage on this salary?"

*Anarkali* I didn't know what it meant. I had not even known what my father was earning and how we were running the house. So I said, "Why not?" I was totally unaware. But it didn't matter, that is the thing. Not that the starting salary was very low because it was quite comfortable for the time that we were in. But it didn't matter. I never felt that oh, my neighbor has this, I should have this too. You see that kind of a thing, I feel, is very important. That you are happy. And as you progress in time and in life, you start getting other things, and you feel that you have been blessed. Because we were not deprived. We didn't go through a hard time. That is another test that a couple has to go through sometimes. Going through jobless days or not having things to eat. So all that we had not experienced, so from that point of view it was smooth sailing for us.

*Suresh* I think then the whole effort was that we have decided to get married. We have to make a success of it. Hurdles come, you jump over them. For instance, I remember I used to love playing badminton. I used to love playing bridge. But these usually run into two or three hours, it's like golfing. If you are a keen golfer, you are out for three hours. And she was not interested in those things. Well, what I am saying is that whatever came we handled it.

*Anarkali* We don't know whether destiny brought us together, but I'm thankful because I feel that I would have been not very happy if there was another kind of a person with whom I had to get along with. I have been lucky, I found a partner who agrees with most of my thoughts. And I'm proud of his values and the principles that he has. You see, that matters a lot. I could have been married to a husband whose principles were not high at all. And I wouldn't have flourished, and my personality wouldn't have flowered. I wouldn't have had the intellectual inputs that I have had because I have been married to him. So I'm thankful. Otherwise, I would have been miserable if I had been married to somebody else who was not really alike in thoughts and deeds.

*Suresh* Everything flows out of marriage. All these years I've lived with her, and I can't conceive of it without her.

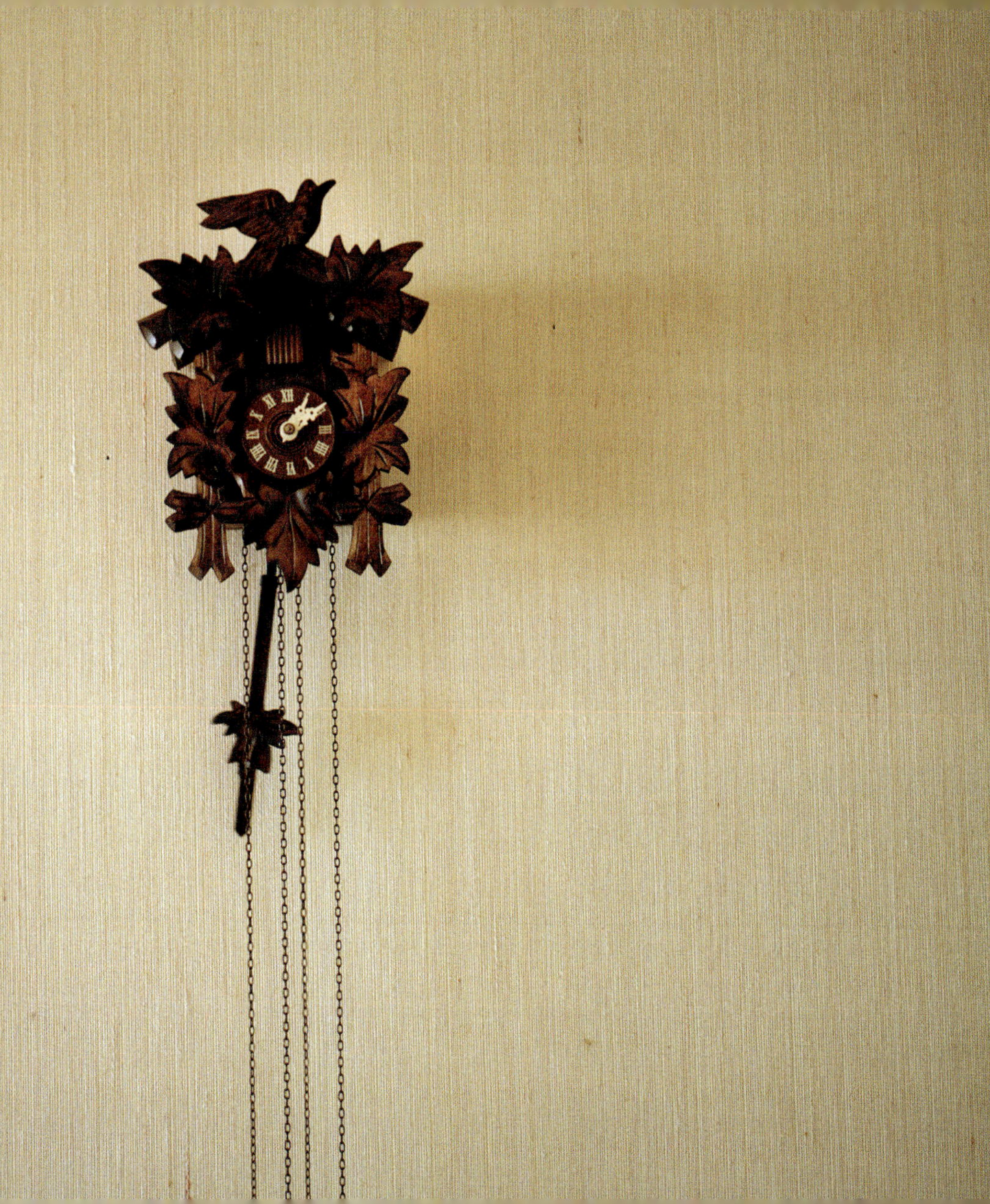

## Arnold and Lorlee Tenenbaum

Savannah, Georgia
Married on June 14, 1959



*Arnold* When you're young, I think, you're very idealistic. You say there is one person in the world I'm gonna meet that's gonna click, and we're just going to live this wonderful life, happily ever after. And in my opinion that's really not true. There are a lot of people that you share interests with, that you care about, that you could probably learn to love. A lot of it's luck too. We met each other at a time when we were both vulnerable and thinking about the possibility of getting married. We shared interests, we shared family values. And it's worked for 50 something years, but that doesn't mean that it could have only have worked with Lorlee or for her that it could only have worked with me. But it's an effort to stay married. It's just not a little bit of fairy dust that someone sprinkles over you, and all of a sudden the world is bright and wonderful and perfect. It's a lot of years of a lot of trials and tribulation and joy and happiness. We don't have any magic formulas. We've gone to bed angry before. And you know, sometimes you pout for two or three days. But that gets less and less as you get older. In the relationship you find out what's important and what isn't.

Our life was our marriage. When we first got married, we thought we were the perfect couple. You know, smart, well educated, good backgrounds, and we were just going to produce little clones. The only person who got cloned is me because I now weigh about twice as much as I did when I got married. But you realize the minute you have a child that they are their own people. There were no clones. At one stage, about 10 or 11 years ago, we started taking some trips to some fairly exotic locations. And every time we took a trip, I wrote a letter that I put in my desk to all the kids to only be opened if we didn't return that said to them you know, don't be concerned about us, we're doing what we wanted to do. We had a wonderful life. But let our legacy to you be that the four of you continue to be close and that you always get along and that was the most important thing to us. So the letters are still sitting here unopened, happily, but they know the message anyhow.

One of the pleasant experiences we wanted to mention was that we had a very direct connection to the movie The

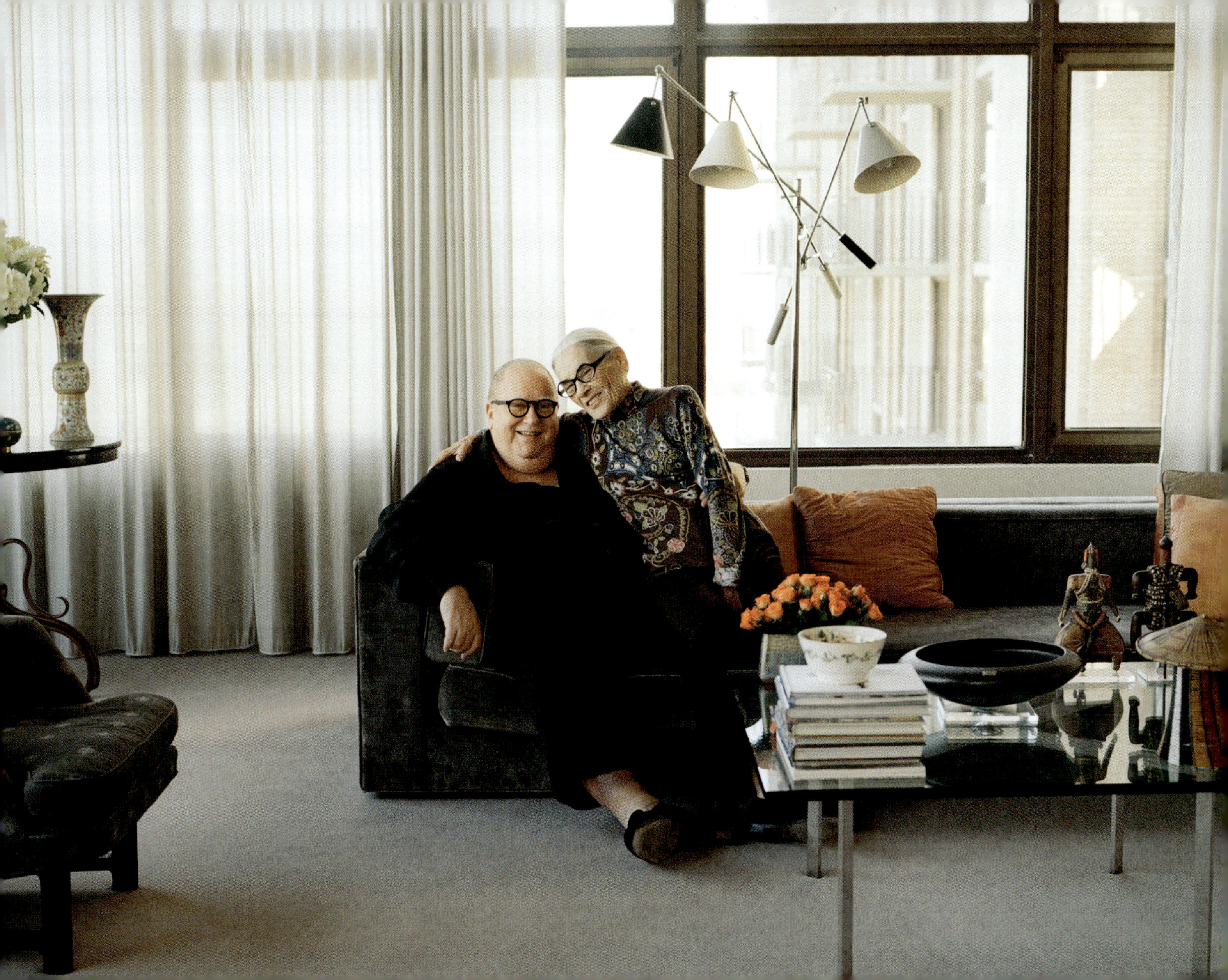

Royal Tenenbaums. It was not about our family. They were, if you've seen the movie, a family of really quirky geniuses. We have very bright kids, and they are slightly quirky but not as quirky as they were in the movie. But although the movie was not about us, there was a few references that were unique to our family that sort of among ourselves we could chuckle about. One was that Gwyneth Paltrow's name was Margot, and we have a Margot Tenenbaum. Another was that Owen went away to rehab in North Dakota, and that was a reference to Lorlee being from North Dakota. We had fun being a part of it in our own very remote way, and since then our name recognition has improved a thousand percent. Especially with young people. So that's that story. For our 40th wedding anniversary the kids had a poster of The Royal Tenenbaums framed for us that they got from Wes Anderson, and he inscribed it to the real royal Tenenbaums. But the tag line in the poster is *Family is a Sentence, Not a Word.* And that says an awful lot. The love and the marriage and hopefully the family if that's what you choose to have turns out not to be a sentence but a lifetime of good experiences. That's what we're all about.

We've really had a fairly prosaic life in many ways. But we've been blessed with the ability to travel, with kids who were good and caring, and a lot of our pleasure comes from them. And we still care about each other. We know who likes privacy and who doesn't want to talk in the morning, and you know, all of those things. And we love our peace and quiet and our own routine. And our intention is just to keep on living until it's over.

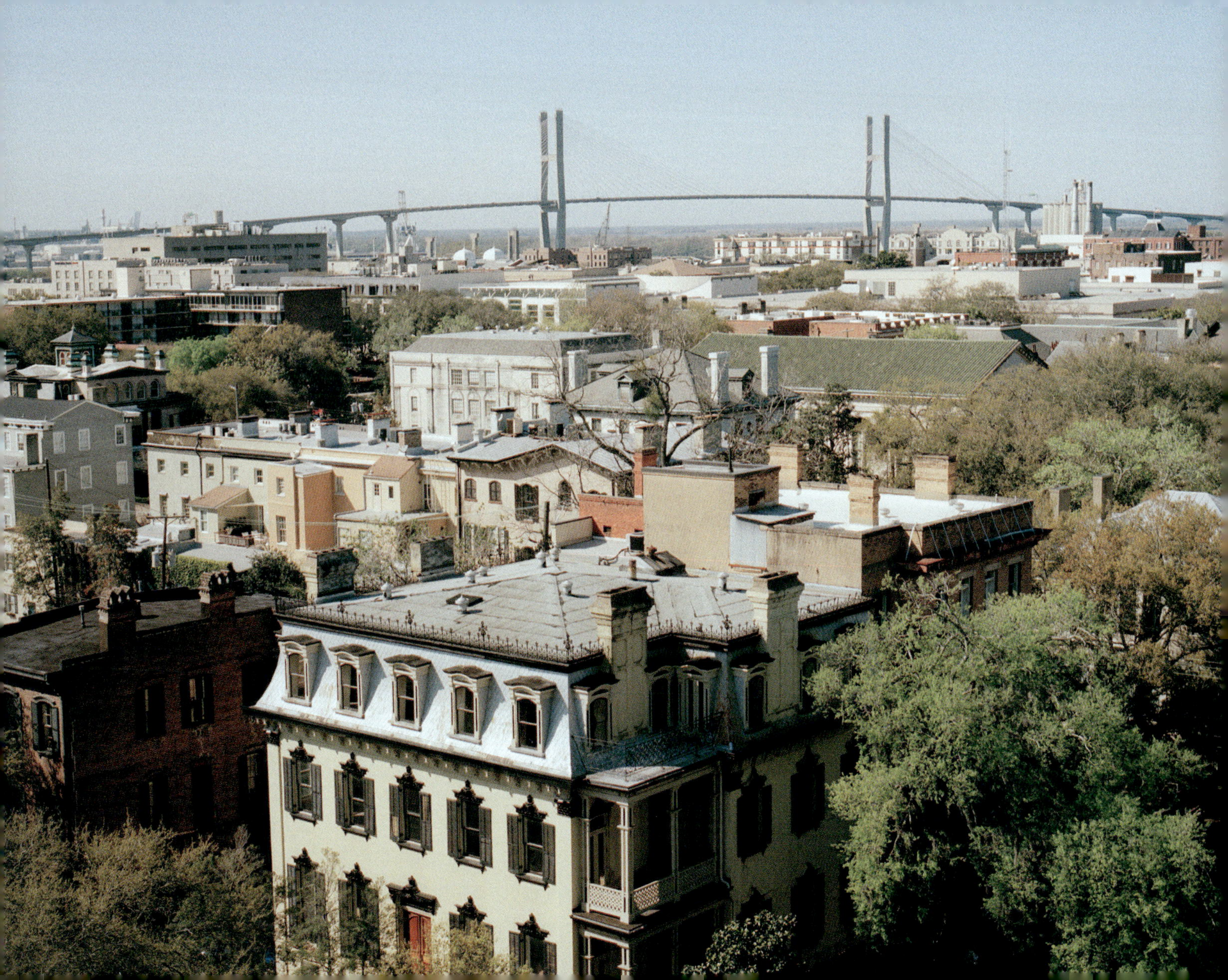

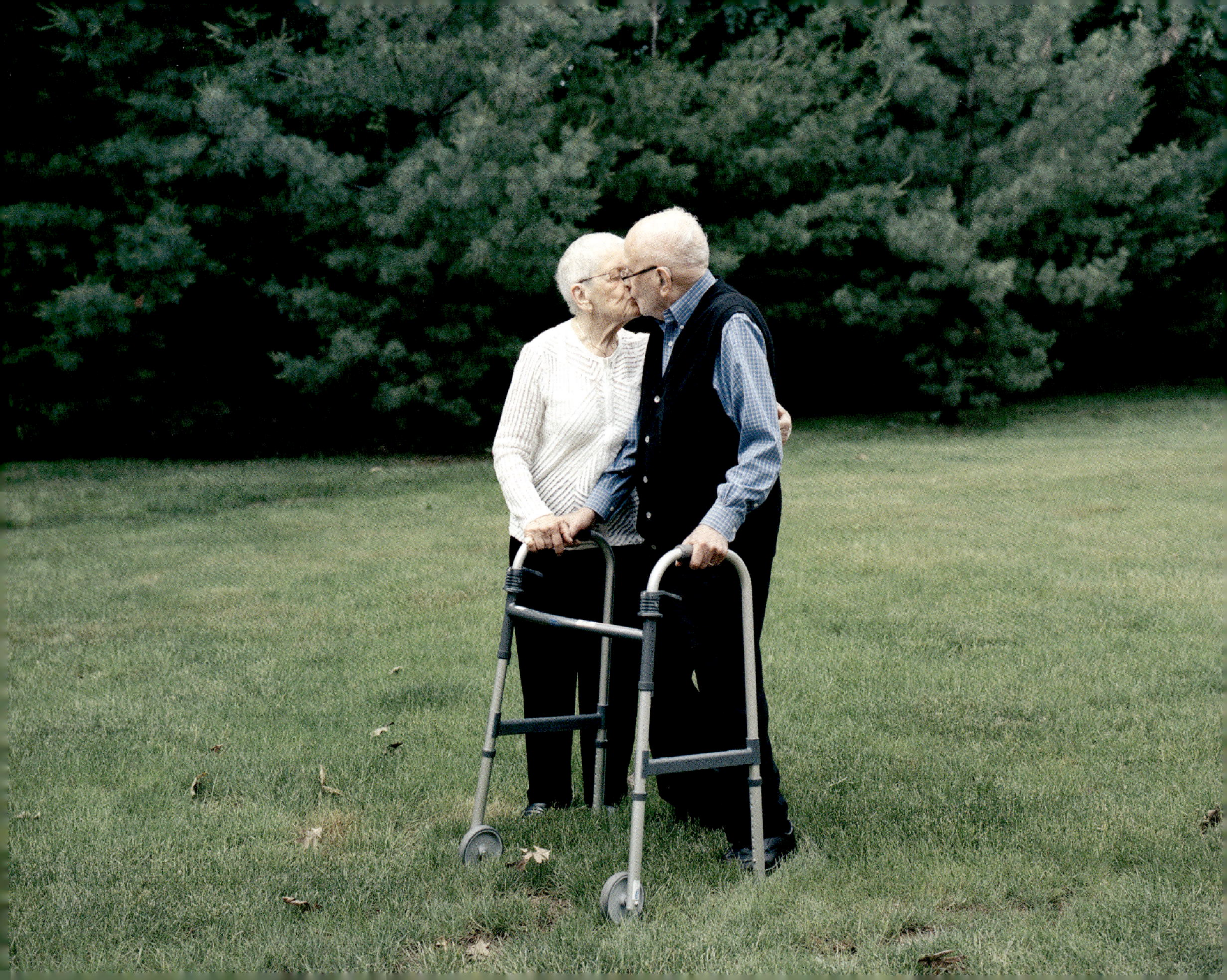

# Joseph and Dorothy Bolotin

Sharon, Pennsylvania

Married on June 16, 1938

*Dorothy* He was in a fraternity, and he said to another fellow, "You have to toss a coin, and one of us is going to get this younger sister." And they tossed a coin and he won. He won me! And I was 15 and a half years old when I met him. He was a sophomore in college, and I was a sophomore in high school. And that's how we met.

It was during the deep Depression and I can still remember that he invited me to go to a dance later on and I said, "I can't go because I don't have anything to wear." And my sister was at the bottom of the stairs, and she was yelling, "We'll find something. We'll find something! Don't say no! Do go!" So I said, "Well, I guess I can go if we find something to wear." So I found a dress. It must have belonged to my sister and my aunt lived with us and she had a skunk coat. Skunk was very popular at the time. And I wore her skunk coat, and I had earrings on. And I went off to the dance with Joe in this outfit. I guess the clothes don't make a difference, actually. It didn't make any difference whether I had the brand new dress on or whether I had an old dress on. But I did go to the dance.

I was very young, and did girls my age date? Not like they do today. You know at 13 they are grown up and trying to be their mothers. It wasn't like that when I was growing up. I remember I was 12 or 13, and you can believe it or not, but I was wearing long underwear. Underwear down to the ankle. And one day I turned to my mother and said, "I am not going to wear this anymore." And with that I took the scissors and I cut the legs off. They would laugh today if I showed up in long underwear. But young people are different today. I don't know if they are as sophisticated as they'd like me to think they are. But they are much more grown up. So I was very unsophisticated.

It's a process—love. It's a gradual process of you're very nice and I like you very much and then pretty soon it's I like you a lot. I couldn't pinpoint any moment in our romance where I said, "Oh my God, I'm madly in love with this man." I wasn't madly in love with him. But it was a process of growing into it. Feeling very comfortable with each other, which is more important. I had to finish my education and he had to finish medical school, so it was just a long time. I guess I was willing to wait. We went together almost seven years, and that's a long time to date somebody. I think it was a true romance.

In June we will have been married for 74 years. I never think of it in terms of years. I think of it in terms of good years. In love, hot romance doesn't last forever. Then you have children pretty soon, and you get interested in what your children are doing. And now, really, very honestly, I'm a caregiver to a man who takes care of himself pretty much by himself, but he couldn't live without me. If it weren't me, it would have to be somebody else. So I would say that yes, I think love changes. I would say we're still in love. We still love each other. It's focusing, doing little things. He's an amazing man.

I don't know what it would be like having loved somebody else. I never loved anybody else. And I wonder what love means to many people. I'm afraid it doesn't mean the same thing to them as it does to me. I think it has to do with good times and bad times. They are not all good and they are not all bad and you can't get mad every time it's bad because you get over it. I don't know what the word love means to you, but to me it means stability and the ability to get along through the bitter and the better and it's not wild. It's not something that's exciting every day. Maybe sort of tranquil. It's easygoing. Exciting love I wouldn't be able to tell you about. I don't know what it's like. Maybe you can tell me.

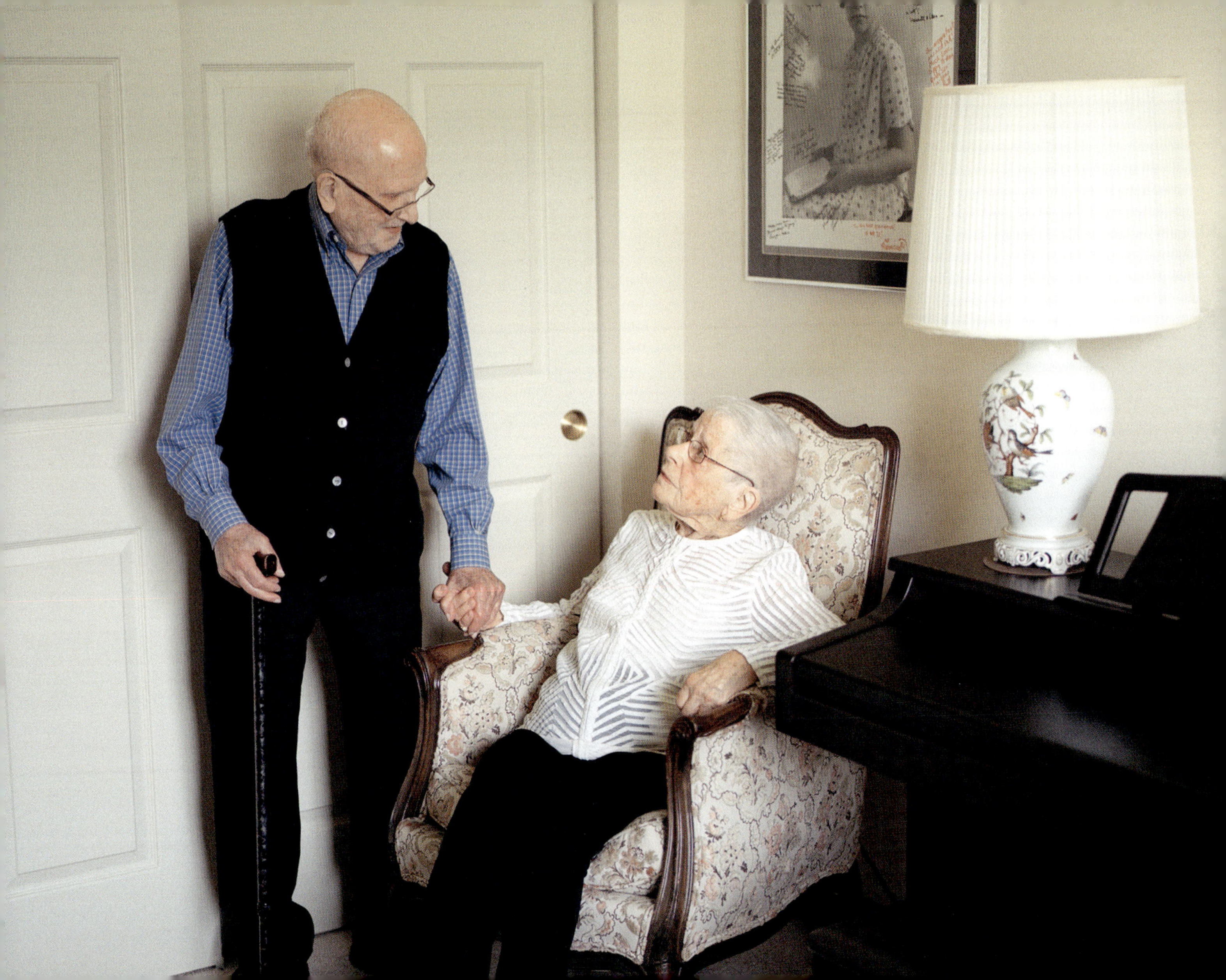

## Moses "Moe" and Tessie Rubenstein

Brooklyn, New York
Married on June 21, 1942



*Moe* When you're young, it's a different type of love than the love we feel now. This is a mature love. That was a young love. It's like a young wine and a mature wine. And in the beginning, of course, there's a sexual attraction, but right now sex has very little to do with it. But we love each other very much. Every day my wife expresses her love to me. "Did I tell you how much I love you today?" Every day. Every day she says that.

*Tessie* Whenever we decide to do anything, we always discuss it beforehand. We never argue with each other. We always discuss things for positive and for negative aspects, and we decide which way we should go. Which would be best for us. And it works out that way. Then you don't argue and you don't use bad language and you don't annoy one another. But you're kind to one another, and your interest is to make your mate pleased with you and content. I even ask him what he would like to eat, and I give him a choice so that he can have what he likes.

*Moe* She was a home economics teacher. Naturally, I eat very well. I'm a good eater.

*Tessie* But you don't show it with heavy weight.

*Moe* Oh, I'm not too heavy. I maintained the same weight that I had in the army. I got out I was 165 pounds. Now I weigh 165, sometimes a little less. But she loves me anyway no matter what I weigh. Don't you dear?

*Tessie* Yes, I do.

*Moe* Good. Well, what else can we say? Love is a matter of being respectful to each other. It's a matter of considering, consideration of one another and considering their feelings. Not you do this and I do that. We do things together. When we were younger, I was working most of the time, seven days a week in hospitals, and it was hard to be very loving to one another. I never saw her. But now we see each other all day long. We're never out of each other's sight. When I was in the hospital, she couldn't sleep because I wasn't near her. She has to know that I'm next to her.

*Tessie* Close by, close by. And we sleep in two separate beds. It isn't like we're in one bed.

*Moe* It's actually two single beds that are very close together. It's bigger than a king-sized bed.

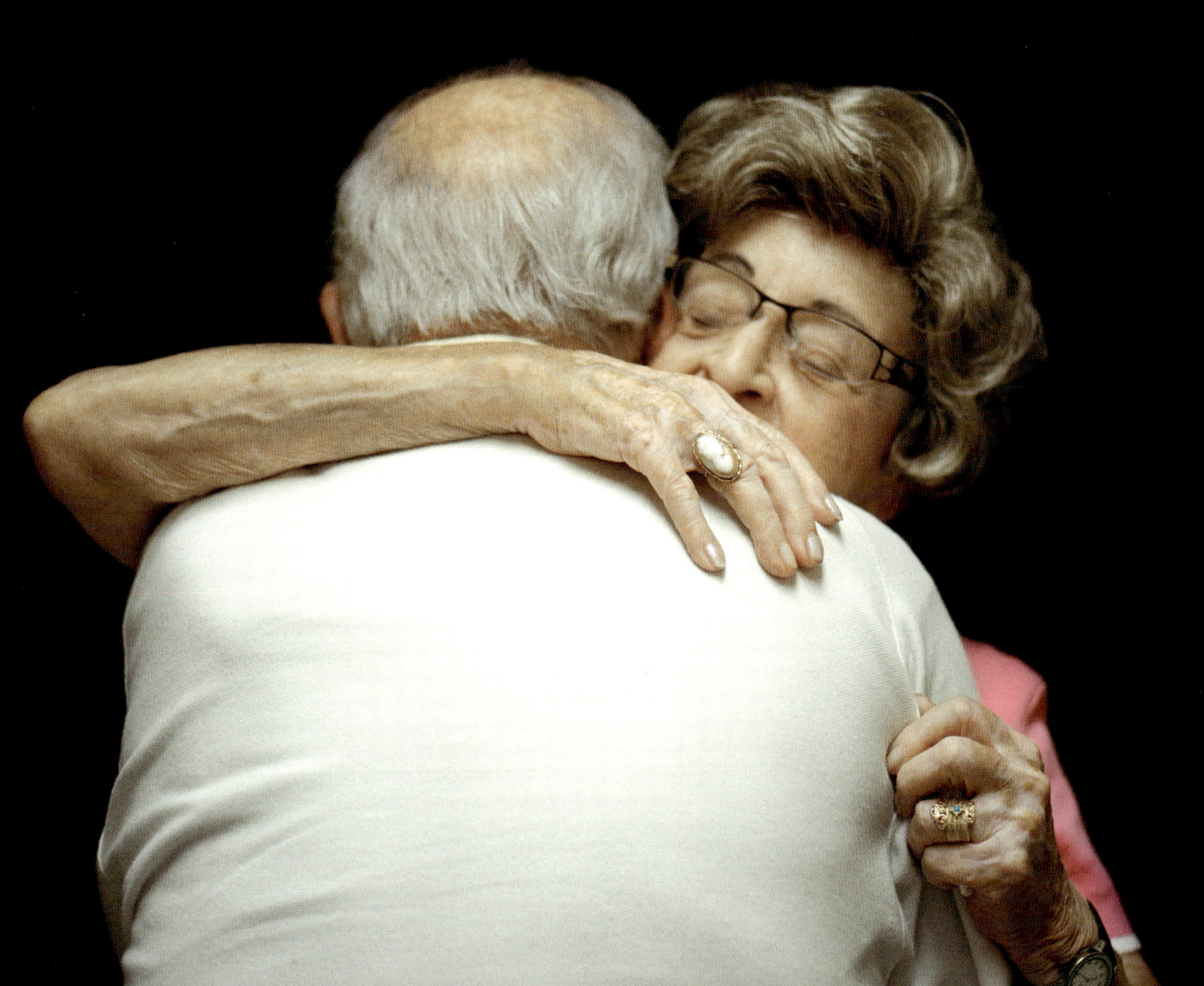

*Tessie* We had it made to order.

*Moe* But we're near each other. I could put out my hand, that's how I know she's not out of her bed at night. She likes to wander now. I'm a very light sleeper anyway, I hear grass growing. And I worry about her, I worry about her very much. How about you? You worry about me?



*Tessie* I think about you all the time.

*Moe* Now I'm going on 88, my wife is 85, and I'm only wishing for another five or six years of life. This is all we want. We don't want to live much longer. We'd like to see our grandchildren get married and be happy like we were. As a matter of fact, I always say to my wife, "I wish I could reach 94." That's the aim of my existence. And I'd hate to leave my little wife here. And she'd hate to leave me.

## Guillermo "Willy" and Balbina Lopez

Tampa, Florida

Married on October 26, 1952

*Willy* Originally, this house was $9,200. The payments were $39 a month, and I told her, "How are we gonna pay that?" But we did it.

*Balbina* People nowadays don't believe the mortgage was $39. My husband used to work at American Can. He worked there for 30 years. And he used to work from 3:30 p.m. to 12 a.m. so that he could take our daughters to school and bring them home. I got up about three o'clock in the morning to make my food for the day and put Willy's separate, so he could eat before he went to work. I used to be petrified, scared to stay alone at night.

*Willy* Sometimes I'd work the midnight shift, 12 a.m. to 7 a.m. I liked that one because it was only six and a half hours, and they pay you for eight. But I was never here.

*Balbina* At least he took the girls to school. I never had to worry.

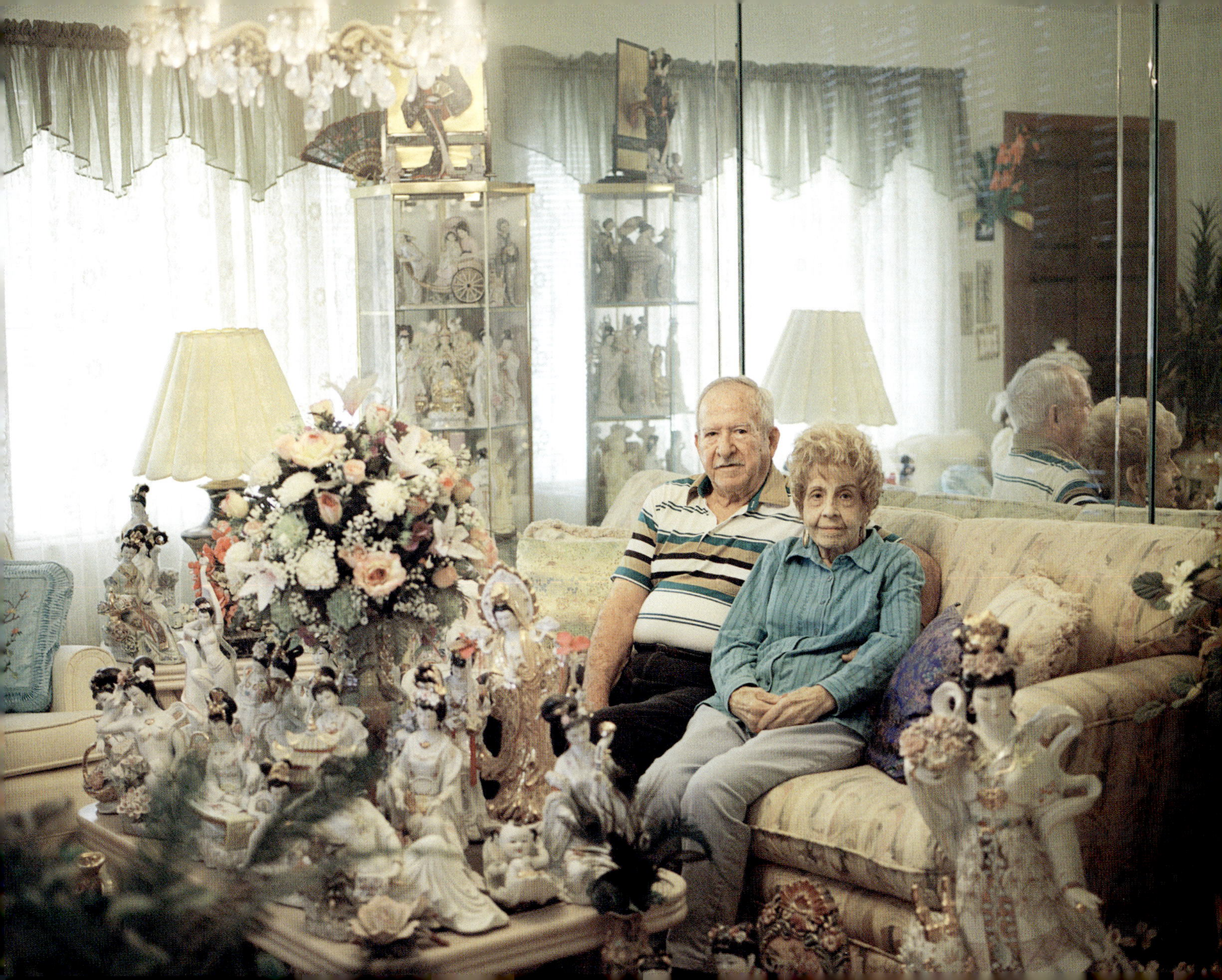

*Willy* I don't know where the 60 years went—they went by so fast. We used to get mad at each other—that happens all the time. She never got mad. I did. When you go to bed, you have to forget about what happened. Don't go to bed mad. And we always worked it out, but we had our ups and downs.

*Balbina* And I read in Ann Landers about a lady who said never go to bed mad cause the next morning you don't know. She said she had an argument with her husband and didn't talk to him, and he died that night. And I said uh, oh. That's not going to happen to me. It's been so long that I practically know what he's going to do. Or he knows what I am going to do. It's amazing. I remember my dad and my mom—my mother was 96 and my dad was 93 when he died. And it was very emotional for my mom. I made my mother come here because I didn't want her living there by herself. I don't think I could live now if he would be gone.

*Willy* We do everything together. Whatever she wants to do, I go along with it. Every Sunday we go to church. I look now— she is 82 and I'm 80—you look at what is coming in the future when she's gone or I'm gone. I wish we would go both together. When we die, the same day for both of us. Not to be with one gone and the other has to be alone.

*Balbina* When I think about it then, I cry all day. We're supposed to be happy, but we're just so used to being together. I'm retired, he's retired. If he's sick, I take care of him, and if I'm sick, he takes care of me.

*Willy* Marriage has been beautiful. Ups and downs sometimes. The main thing I learned through the years was that she was like my mother. Very caring and taking care of everything. I didn't have to worry about other things. And I respected her, and I kept true to her. When we lived in my mother-in-law's house, there wasn't a problem when I got laid off because there was always food on the table. But when we moved into our own house, we were on our own, and sometimes we had a strike. Like I told you before, the mortgage was $39, and I said, "How are we going to pay that?"

But we did it. Working together, taking care of the bills, taking care of the kids. My mother always told me when I was a kid, "You don't learn anything bad in church. Nothing." Religion has done a lot to keep us together. You learn from older people, how they get along and everything. If they believe in something, don't take it away from them. Don't make them change because you don't like it.

*Balbina* I think that God put us together, really.

*Willy* Respect each other, don't go to bed mad and forget what happens and work it out.

For instance, I go along with my wife's collections. Why am I going to take this away from her? A lot of men would not allow this. But that's her hobby. That's what she likes, and as long as she takes care of me, I accept it. I told her we had too much, but we work on it. If she's a good person, a good wife, a good mother, you accept whatever turns her on. A lot of them I bought for gifts or birthdays. She loves it. We stopped buying them 10 or 15 years ago. The only place left is on top of my head.

## Jim and Marilyn Lovell

Horseshoe Bay, Texas
Married on June 6, 1952



*Marilyn* When I married Jim, it wasn't even in the big picture that he would be a test pilot, that he would fly fighter flights and that he would eventually become an astronaut. I would go down to the space shuttle launches and I'd take the children with me and it was just exhilarating to know that he was going up and doing what he wanted to do. So it was just a very exciting life, it really was. There were many times that it was worrisome—especially with Apollo 13. I was more concerned at that point about the children than I was about myself because of his life being in danger.

I would say I was always apprehensive for what he was going to do, but for some reason or another when he went up in Apollo 8, I was so excited for him that he was going to be one of the first men to go around the moon. But when it came to Apollo 13, that was his fourth mission, I didn't like the number 13. I was very nervous about it all, but I kept it to myself. That's one thing that the astronaut wives did, you kept everything to yourself. And I think most military wives did that too. I think being in the military really prepared me to be an astronaut's wife. It was similar in a way because there were about eight years that he would leave on Sunday night and not come home until Friday. So he was gone all the time, and I was the head of the household. Paid the bills, took care of the children. Just responsible for the house and everything and just took over. With Apollo 8, he went up at Christmas time, which was disturbing in a way in the beginning because the family was planning on going to Acapulco, Mexico.

*Jim* Well, the mission changed. We were supposed to go around the Earth, but then we had a fire on another spacecraft. And then we heard two things. One, that the Russians were going to send people to circumnavigate the moon and come back. Then, our lunar module, which we were going to test in Earth orbit, was not ready. So they changed the mission of Apollo 8—from Earth orbit to lunar flight, including orbiting the moon and coming back again. And so when we prepared for this flight, and we were looking at the times that we could launch, it turned out that we were going to launch on the 21st of December, which meant that we would go into lunar orbit

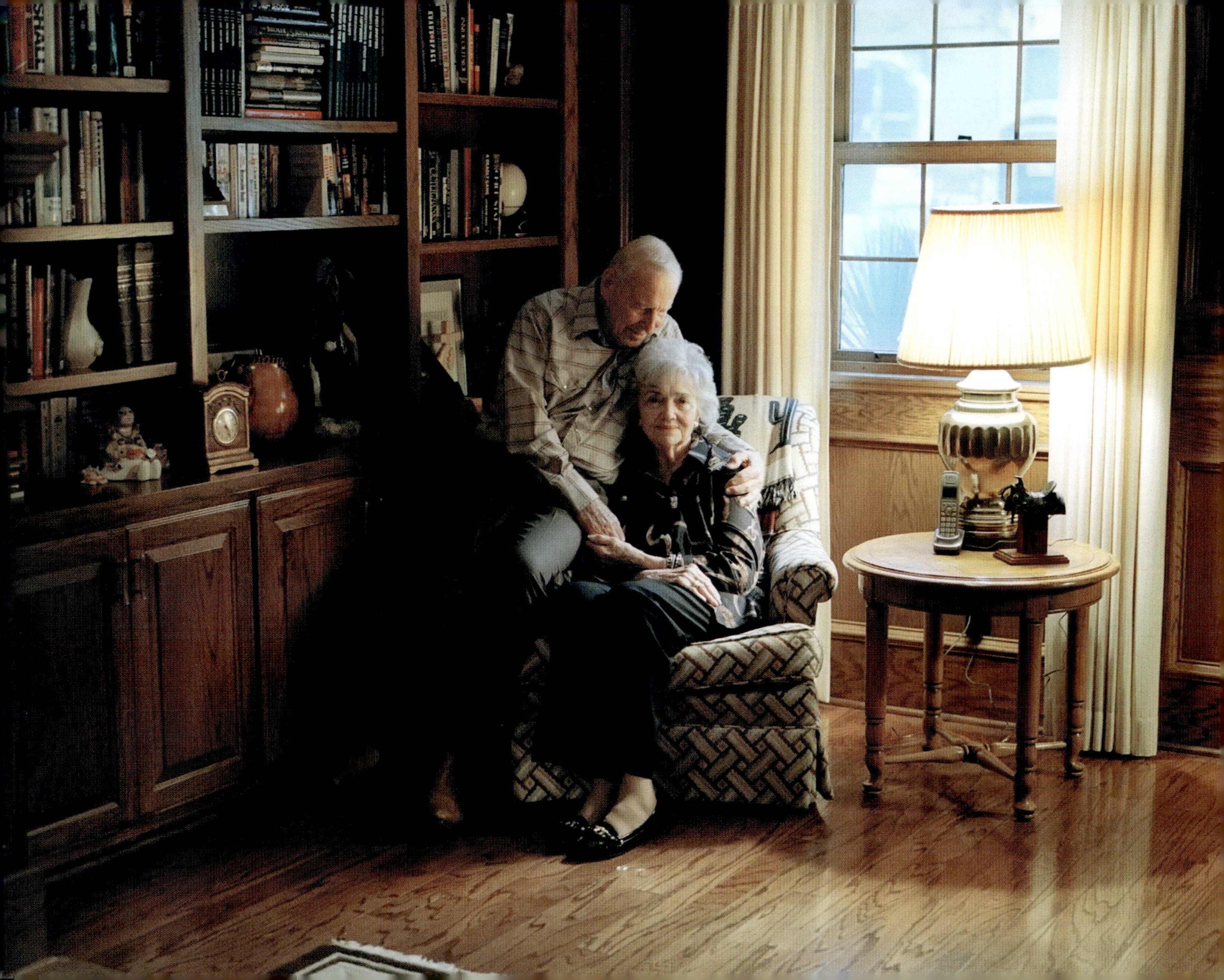

on Christmas Eve. And consequently, all this sort of came up, and then when I found out that I was going to the moon, then I thought, well, what can I do? I won't be here for Christmas. She always wanted a mink coat.

*Marilyn* What lady wouldn't?

*Jim* She was always looking for a mink coat, never could afford one. But then I knew at Neiman Marcus, a big department store, one of the Marcus brothers, Lawrence Marcus. So before the flight I went down there. And I said, "Look, I think I can afford this little mink jacket," and he said, "OK." But I said, "I want it delivered on Christmas morning." So I wrote a note in the jacket.

*Marilyn* "Merry Christmas from the man on the moon. Love, Jim."

*Jim* So what Lawrence Marcus did was when we were flying, a chauffeur came up to the house with a package.

*Marilyn* He came up in a Rolls-Royce, and he came to the door and NASA had security there, of course, and they let me talk to him. And they handed me this beautiful package, which was wrapped in blue foil. And on top of it, it had the Earth and the moon, and it had a spacecraft that looked like it was going around the moon. It was just fabulous. When I opened up the package, I just didn't know what was happening. And it was all light blue tissue paper with little silver stars and I pulled out this mink jacket and I mean, absolutely, I screamed, of course. I couldn't believe it. And, of course, I saw the note from Jim. I mean, that was very romantic, that he thought of me enough to know that I should be remembered in some way —very special for Christmas. Another thing that he has done over the years in the space program was that he named a mountain for me, Mount Marilyn. And which to this day, it's still carrying that name. No one has ever taken it away.

*Jim* The astronomical union, who names craters after ancient philosophers and scientists, never bothered to name the mountain, so I named it. They refused to formally recognize it, but informally— you could Google it if you so desire, Mount Marilyn.

*Marilyn* It's a little triangle mountain in the front of the moon. He came to see me the night before he took off again, and he showed me a picture. He said, "I am going to name this mountain for you," and I thought, you're kidding. I couldn't believe he was going to do that.

*Jim* It was in our flight path around the moon, so we could see it easily.

*Marilyn* In fact, when Neil Armstrong landed on the moon, he used that as one of his last checkpoints before he landed. So I heard him say it on TV when I was watching all this, and I just couldn't believe it. In the meantime, just recently for my birthday last year, Jim had a print of it framed, and he has a little plaque on it saying what mountain it is. So that was very romantic. He's done a lot of things, very thoughtful things like that.

*Jim* Now you see one of the downsides of being married so long is the fact that you run out of good ideas for presents. I mean, what else can you give her?



*Marilyn* Most men wouldn't do that. To me, it's very thoughtful.

## Martin and Ruth Spencer

Brooklyn, New York
Married on October 25, 1942



*Martin* I have a wife today that I really had when I was 22 years old. I'm telling you the truth. We never fight about anything that has any consequence. It's always a trivial matter. But it doesn't mean anything to us because we always kiss and make up before we go to bed, and we always get up in the morning. I think it was her sacrificing her way of life for me so that we could have a family and live the way we are. I'm not trying to be a big shot, I'm telling you the truth. We had lots of friends who went the other way because they couldn't control themselves, so they walked out. And I say I've got the best wife in the world, why should I go anyplace else?

I believe that everybody when they are born, they are a half a person. And when they meet their other half, they become a whole person. She had what I needed. And we're two whole people now.

*Ruth* There was a time in my life when I was a little bit younger I would say to myself, who am I? I'm Marty's wife, I am Marc's mommy, Roger's mommy, but who am I? And then you say, well, on the other hand you're very lucky to be Marty's wife and Marc's mommy.

I think today is very different. Many young ladies want a career, they want to be able to say I can do. In my generation that wasn't so and many, many marriages were horrible, but the women were stuck there because they didn't have the resources to go out on their own. I wouldn't have had the courage, I know that myself if it was so bad, I don't know what I would have done. After you step out of a marriage, especially with children, you've got to be able to support them.

When we were much younger, Marty said to me, "I don't care what you do all day long, but I want to know that you are home at three o'clock when the kids come home from school so they know you're there." We lived on 15th Street and Avenue R. There was a little street, it was a dead-end street, and I would say all the houses on the street had kids about the same age. We'd get up really early in the morning, all the mommies, do whatever you had to do in the house—straighten it out, fix dinner—and then we sat and played Canasta or Mahjong. But at 2:30 we were finished. Everybody was back in their own house at a quarter to three so that when the kids came home you were there for them. I remember resenting the fact that my mom used to go to the office with my dad and she'd leave notes when you come

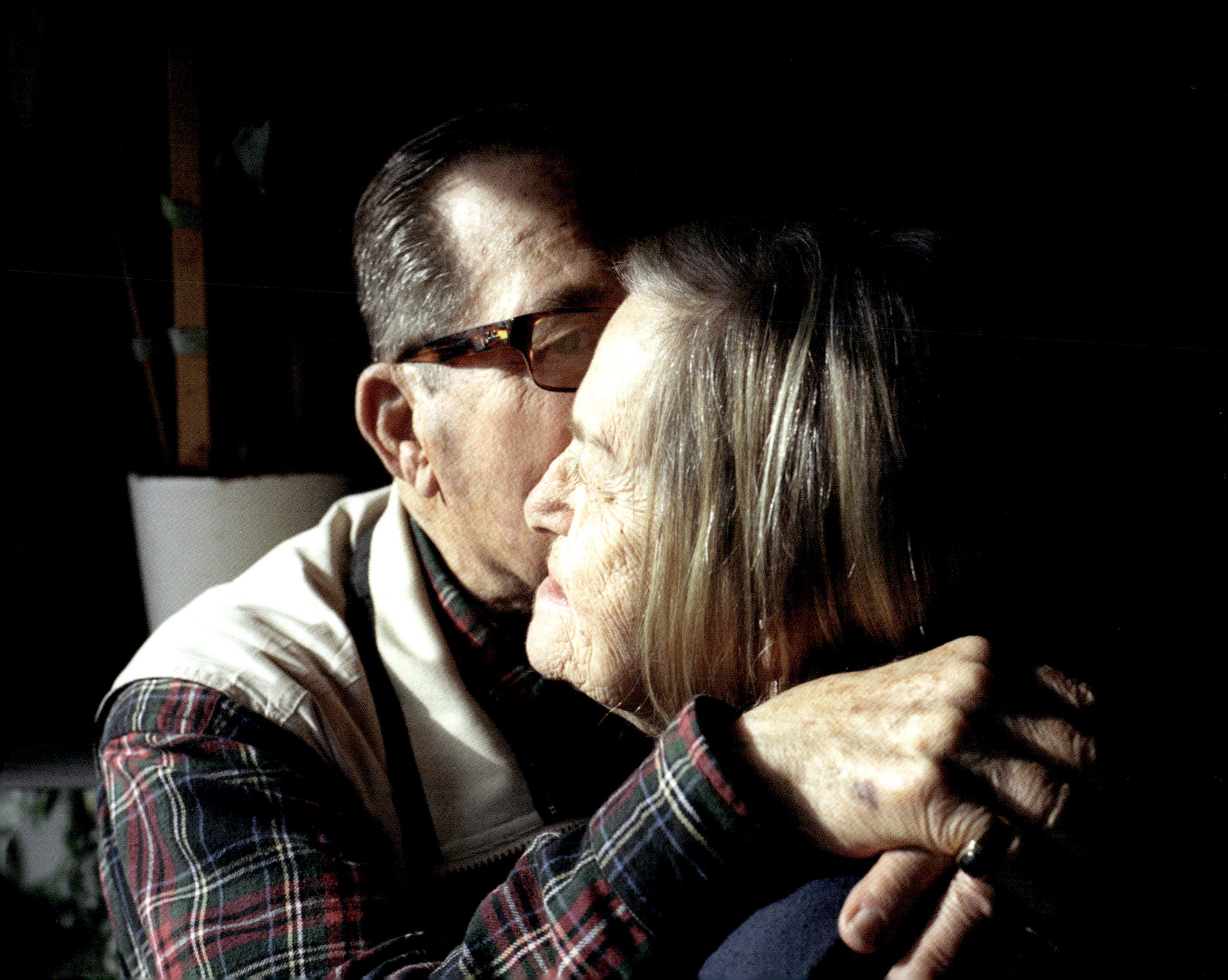

home from school—peel potatoes and set the table. And yet today it's normal. The kids are accustomed to it. Mommy goes to work.

My mother said, "When you get married the most important person in your life is your husband. The children move away." And if you don't have something in common, all of a sudden these years they roll away and who is this stranger sitting in your living room? There are some women where they would kill for their kids and they are the most important. And the husband? If he eats, he eats! But where the kids are concerned, they come first. My mother said don't ever do that. Your husband comes first.



Love gets deeper as you go along. I think that's why so many women when they're widowed later in life go into such a deep depression. Because this is someone who's been with you really all your life. I was 22, I'm married longer than I was single. I say to everybody, I don't even remember being single. I think we were married when we were born!

## Myron "Mike" and Frances Berrick

New York, New York
Married on August 5, 1942

*Frances* We originally moved to this assisted living facility in August. When we walked into the apartment, it was empty, of course, and it was a gorgeous, sunny day and the sun was streaming in here, and we said, "Oh wow." Actually, I said, "Oh wow." My husband came along very reluctantly.

*Mike* We moved after Frances came out of the hospital. She said our house was too big. We had a seven-room house, and even though we had a stair lift, it was hard. It was a wrenching move because I gave up my car and all that, but here we are. The worst part of the move, I think, was all the big black garbage bags filled of stuff that I never threw away. I never threw anything away. I tell people I still have my first wife!

*Frances* I was ready to kill him.

*Mike* She was going to kill me because I don't like to throw things away.

One of the things with us is that we have not accepted

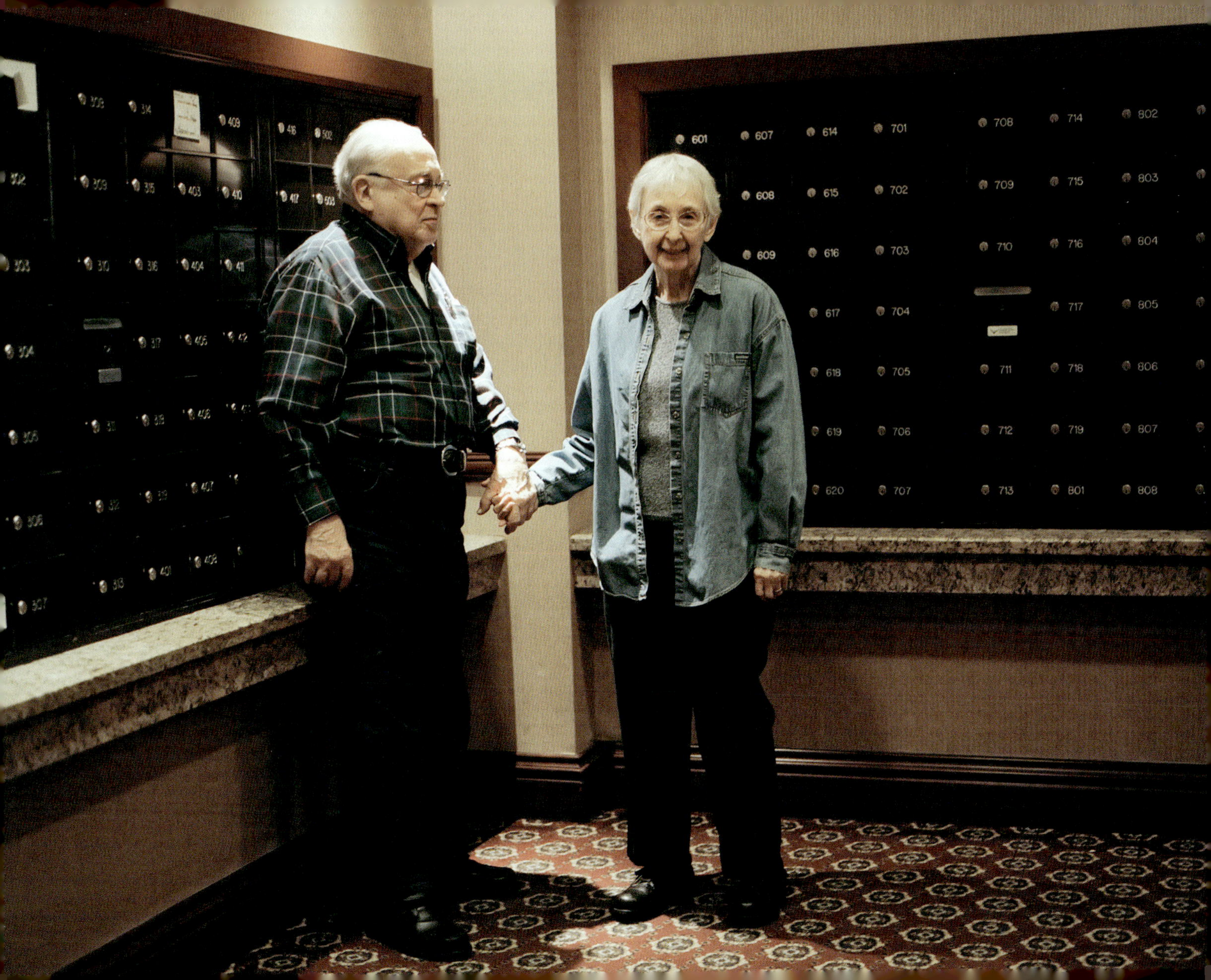
601
607
614
701
708
714
802
608
615
702
709
715
803
609
616
703
710
716
804
617
704
717
805
618
705
711
718
806
619
706
712
719
807
620
707
713
801
808

the fact that we're old. And I resent being old very much. For example, last night we were dancing. I used to be an excellent dancer, and last night I was having trouble not falling down. So these things have sneaked up on Frances and I. We're not what we used to be, but we still think of ourselves that way. I think that helps a great deal because some of the people here think the way we do, and others have given up and are old. It's a real division. I remember back when 80 was considered old. But not anymore.

We originally met at a theater on Kings Highway. Frances was on a date with my friend Teddy, and they had gone to the theater to see *The Great Dictator*. They went as a couple, but I bumped into them. So after the movie we all walked down to an ice cream place called Cohen's on Kings Highway and we were sitting and talking and Teddy, of course, drank all our ice cream sodas and we were busy talking.

Teddy went off to college in Boston, and Frances was going to New York University. I started NYU, and on my first day, I bumped into a friend of mine, Bernice, who was waiting to have lunch with Frances. And so we all had lunch, and after that we started meeting. One thing led to another. That was the beginning of the end and pretty soon she went up to Boston and I said, "You have to tell Teddy." So she did. She told him that she was going with someone else.

*Frances* I didn't tell him who.

*Mike* He called me to find out who, and I said, "It's me," and he said, "Stop kidding. Who is it?" And it took me about three months to convince him it was me. We were on the subway, and I kept saying, "Teddy, Teddy, listen. It's me." And he said, "You?" And I figured, yeah, he's gonna punch me in the mouth...

"I'll give you her pictures."

*Frances* That's Teddy!

*Mike* It turns out love goes in phases. You're madly in love and then you can't stand each other but you have to think of the children and anyway you don't have enough money for anything else and then you become companions. We're fairly good friends for the most part. But I still think she put a hex on me. To the rest of the world, she is sweet, lovely. To me, she can ring my bell faster than anybody else, but it doesn't matter.

*Frances* What would you do without me?

*Mike* I can spot her, and I don't see that well. I can spot her a block away, and before she lost her vision, it was the same thing for her. There's something about us. We're a couple—that's it. And there's no justification for it because we're very different kinds of people—emotionally, politically, everything and yet…

*Frances* I don't know what we would do without each other. It's as simple as that. Mike has gotten to the point where he doesn't remember very much and I have to keep on top of him for things and sometimes when I suggest to him that he has forgotten something, I don't put it politely, which bothers him a little bit.

*Mike* I am still madly in love—I can't help it. There's something about her—when I see her, my stomach flips. I mean, she was sitting with three other women at the breakfast table and I walk in and it's a big dining room and I spot her. And when I see her…when I see her! And sometimes I am very angry with her! But the same thing happens when I see her. I'm still as madly in love with her as when I met her the first night. The first time we started talking, and I was telling her a very sad story, she was the only one who would listen in that way. And it's been like that ever since.

*Frances* It's the same way for me. I can't see well at all. I can't see your face at this moment, but I can recognize him when he's walking through the dining room. I can see him up the block. It's very interesting. There are very few people I recognize anymore when they are more than this far away from me. But I recognize him. It's an attraction. It's 65 years long.

## José and Leila Ramos

Brooklyn, New York
Married on April 16, 1950



*Leila* I want to tell you a story. I don't know if this is the secret to love or not, but we come from a family where both sides were married for a long, long time. For example, I remember my grandparents celebrated a 75-year wedding anniversary when I was 13. All of my family members marry, and they separate only when one dies.

But it's not easy. We have to work hard, and the main thing is to love each other. If a person loves the other, then you can get through anything—good times, bad times. I think this is the way that a relationship can last. When I don't like something, I tell him. If he doesn't like it, he tells me, and we try to fix it.

Many people describe love in different ways. But love is when you feel and you care for a person— not because he's handsome or he has money. Love is only in your heart. Little by little we see the changes in a person, but we don't change in our hearts. That's the way I feel, and I believe he feels the same way. We are always together, in good and bad. When we married, I was only 15. My husband was 19, and he was a father at 20. He was my first love and my last.

*José* We come from Puerto Rico. Her brother came to me one day and said, "Let's go to New York." I said, "No, no." But he said, "Let's go. If you don't like it, we'll come back." Then he stayed one month because he was working, but I wasn't working at that time. He went back and I stayed. I started working with my uncle, which I did for 33 years in the same place. The boss liked me because I was a good worker.

In Puerto Rico we had a small room in my father's house, and our first baby was born there. When the first baby came, things changed a lot. Because you have to share your love. I always told my wife, "Don't let my child fall!" Things like that. Right now my daughter is 58 years old, and I love her just the same. As if she were a baby. She comes here to eat, we fix food for her.

Then we lived in Manhattan when we had our second daughter. We lived in a very little room. So we looked for a bigger room, a furnished room, which was cheaper at that time. I always went to Central Park with my wife and my kids. I went to the swing, the slides and things like that. We always went together.

Sometimes when you love your wife, you don't tell her every day that you love her. You can love her in silence too.

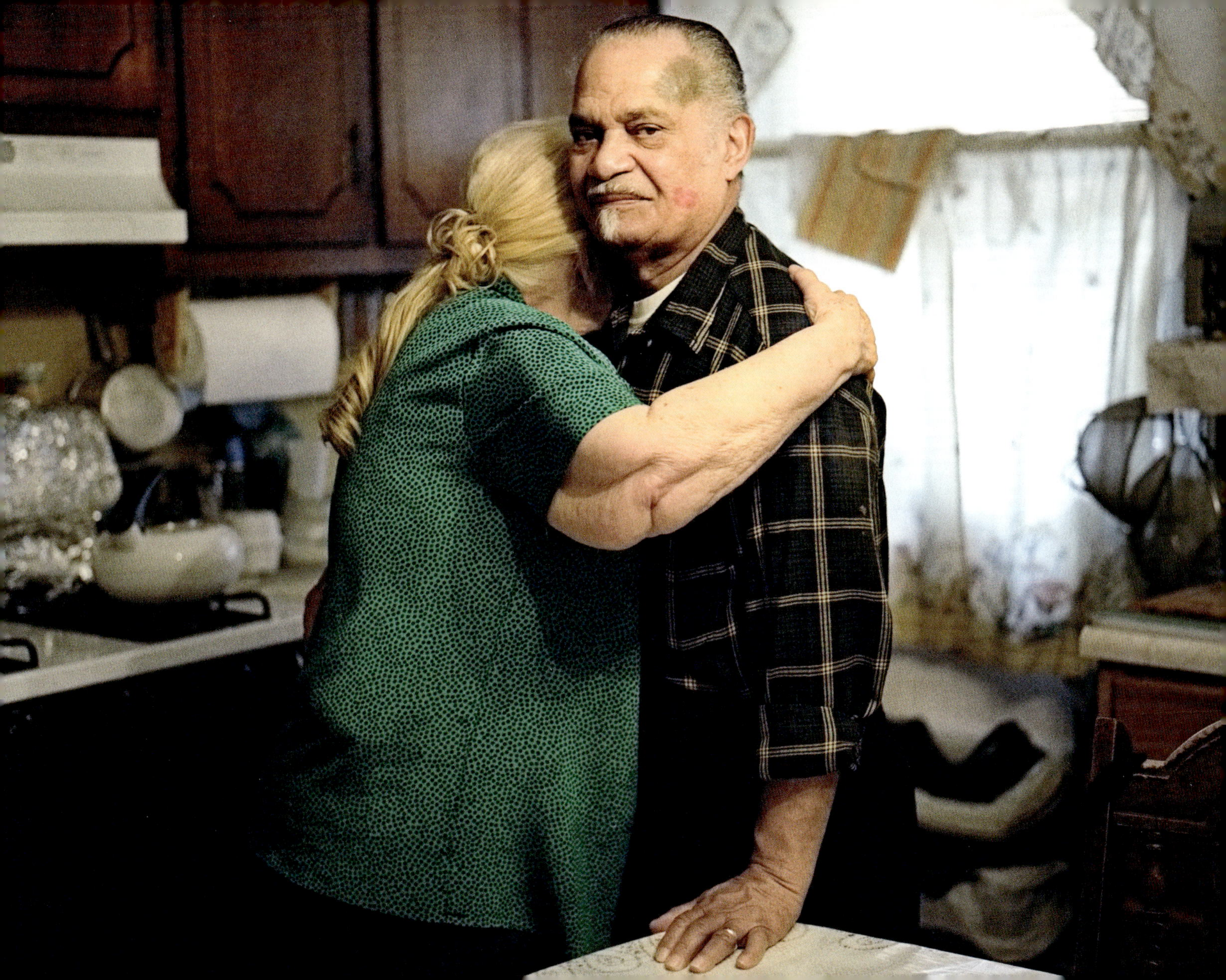

*Leila* But he told me many times that he loves me. I'll say, "How much do you love me?" "Mucho, mucho, mucho." Men are always quieter. That is why many people don't show their love, and that isn't good. Something happens and then they will get divorced and then they say it—*I love you, I love you so much.* Why didn't they say it to begin with? It's one of the secrets too! Tell them that you love them. Some women say, oh my husband doesn't love me, he never told me. That's not good. You have to talk. I know my husband loves me because he's told me many times. My husband is quiet, but he's good.

## Joseph and Norma Vogelman

Great Neck, New York
Married on December 8, 1946

*Norma* We're going to be married 65 years December 8th, so it's a long time. He waited for me to graduate from Brooklyn College. He was already out of the service and working. And he was rich compared to me. I had nothing. I had $42 and a fur coat!

I find I love him more every day. He takes very good care of me. Are you married? You'll find out. These days it's very different. Marriage isn't that important because people live together, and it's very accepted. There is no stigma attached in any way. I mean, look at Andrew Cuomo, a public figure who lives without a marital blessing of any kind. He just lives with another woman, and everybody takes it. He has three children from another marriage, but nobody seems to be upset about it.

My husband is so good to me and he's so handsome and he's really a wonderful person. He has a little problem—he has a short fuse but that comes with age. He's 90 and I'm 86, and we've been together a long time. I don't think either of us would survive without the other. We've been together so many years that we are like one instead of two.

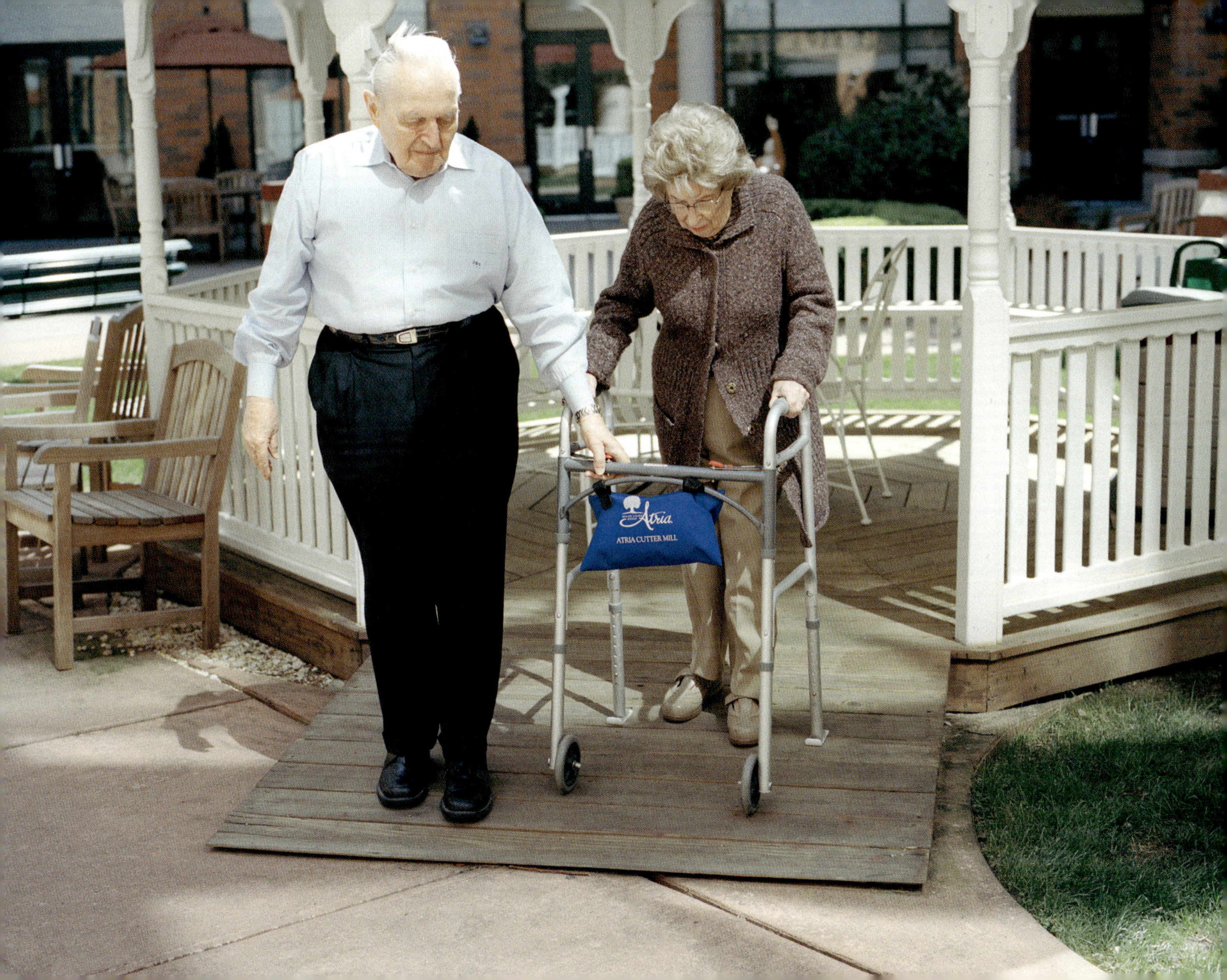
Atria
ATRIA CUTTER MILL

## Samuel and Anna Gorn

Brooklyn, New York
Married on June 8, 1952



*Anna* I met my husband on a holiday in the place where he lived. He told me I even danced with him, but I don't remember this. He is older than me by seven and a half years. My father died when he was 32 years old in the war, and my mother was left at the age of 29 with three children. In Russia you can't do whatever you want like in America. My mother was selling things, and they wanted to put her in jail. Our relatives told my mom to come live with them, and they were in the same town as my husband. Do you know who Stalin is? When Stalin died, they let people out of jail. My mother never was in jail, though, because she hid.

Our relatives said I had to get married because my mother was alone. So I got married to my husband at the age of 17. You might laugh, but in the town where we were married, they don't give gifts. Everyone just sends you a cake. Do you know how many cakes I got? And in June it's hot! So this was my wedding. It was a nice day in the morning. After we got the chuppah outside, it started to rain. I can't even describe how rainy it was. So it was difficult times—a difficult life with money—but we are together.

We argue a lot, but he tells me he loves me anyway. If I'm mad at him, he'll tell me I'm his best friend and that he loves me. I tell him I'm nervous because I have to take a lot of medicine, but at the same time, I try to be nice.

*Samuel* She was a good wife.

*Anna* You see?

When he has a bad time, I am always by his side. But life even if it's bad times or good times, the time goes like water. I don't think if we were in Russia that we could have lived till this age. I know this. A lot of people live there like they did 200 years ago. We've never gone on vacation separately in our life. I need him and he needs me. When I was younger, I told him I would divorce him! Sometimes when I was mad, I would say that because I was young when I married him. But he told me I was a perfect wife.

When we got married, it was one ring for both of us because we couldn't afford another one. So I wore the ring, not him. I wore the ring, and then I gave away my ring to my older son when he got married because he liked it. He still has the ring. I told him to give it back, but he said, "It's mine—for luck." But it wasn't diamonds. It wasn't anything like that.

*Samuel* You're my diamond.

*Anna* Yes, I'm your diamond.

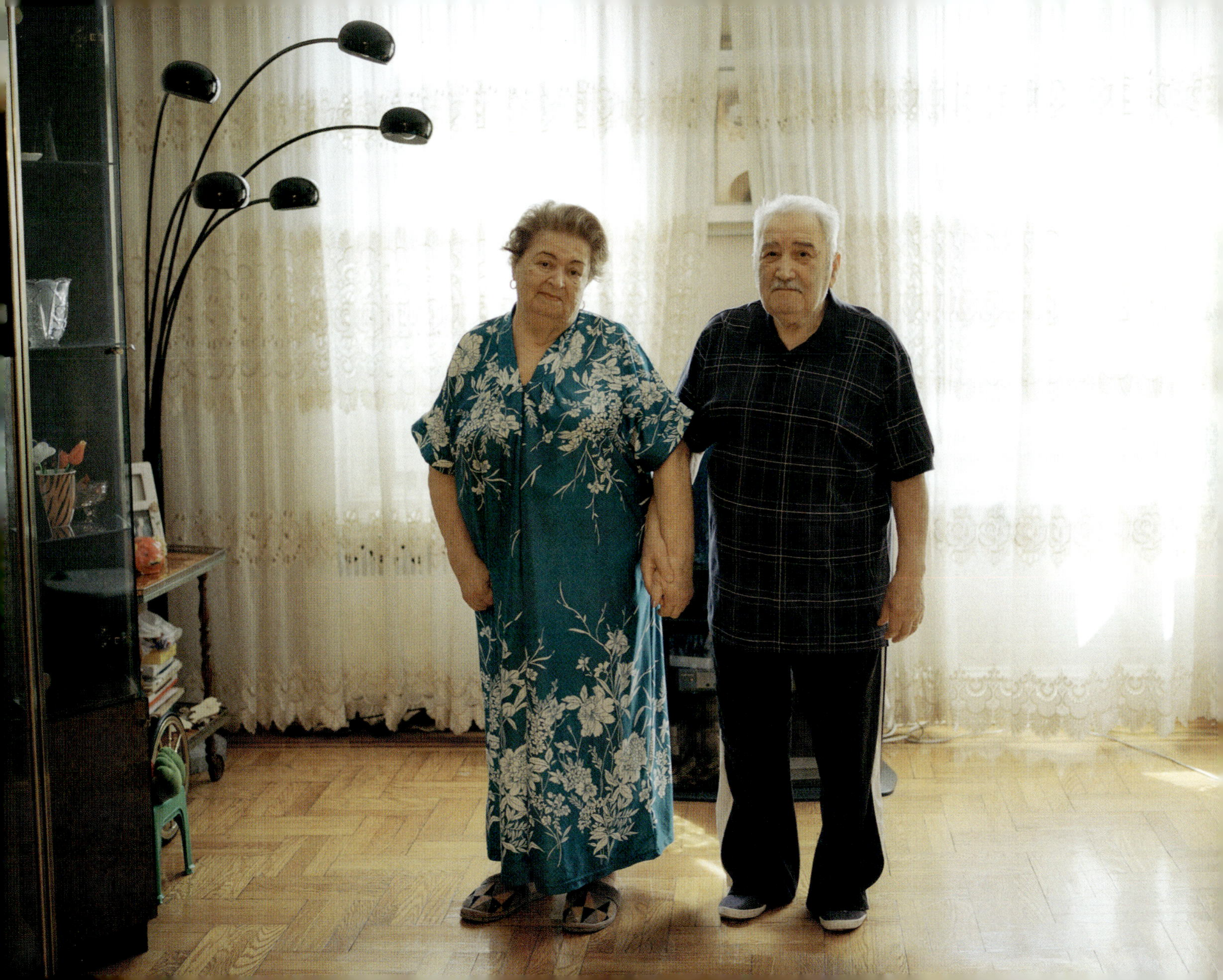

## Milton and Sylvia Zisman

Long Branch, New Jersey
Married on May 27, 1953



*Sylvia* I had my eye on him. He was so good-looking. He had a robust Jewishness about him. At the time there was a very serious struggle of the Rosenbergs, to keep them from being executed. We tried desperately because we believed they were innocent. It was one of the most painful periods. Demonstrations went on for weeks and weeks, and we kind of agreed with each other that we would fight this kind of thing. One thing led to another and we began to go to the demonstrations in Washington and we walked the picket lines. That was our courtship. It was very short because they couldn't wait to execute them. We were married in May, and three weeks later they executed them in June.

Our relationship is based on our struggle to be relevant, to be helpful, to have a shared outlook on life—that gave us the base for our friendship and love. Everything that happened in our domestic life and marriage gave us that opportunity and stability in order to do this. Romance wasn't the first thing on my agenda. Other things came first. I was more down to earth.

We're more old-world types. That's what it was in Europe. The way we are. Romance was a relatively recent accomplishment that we couldn't indulge in. We were working-class people...

What do you think about romance?

*Milton* Growing up in the tiny apartment?

*Sylvia* No, in our relationship. Romance.

*Milton* What about romance? I never thought of it that much.

*Sylvia* He isn't romantic. I'm more romantic.

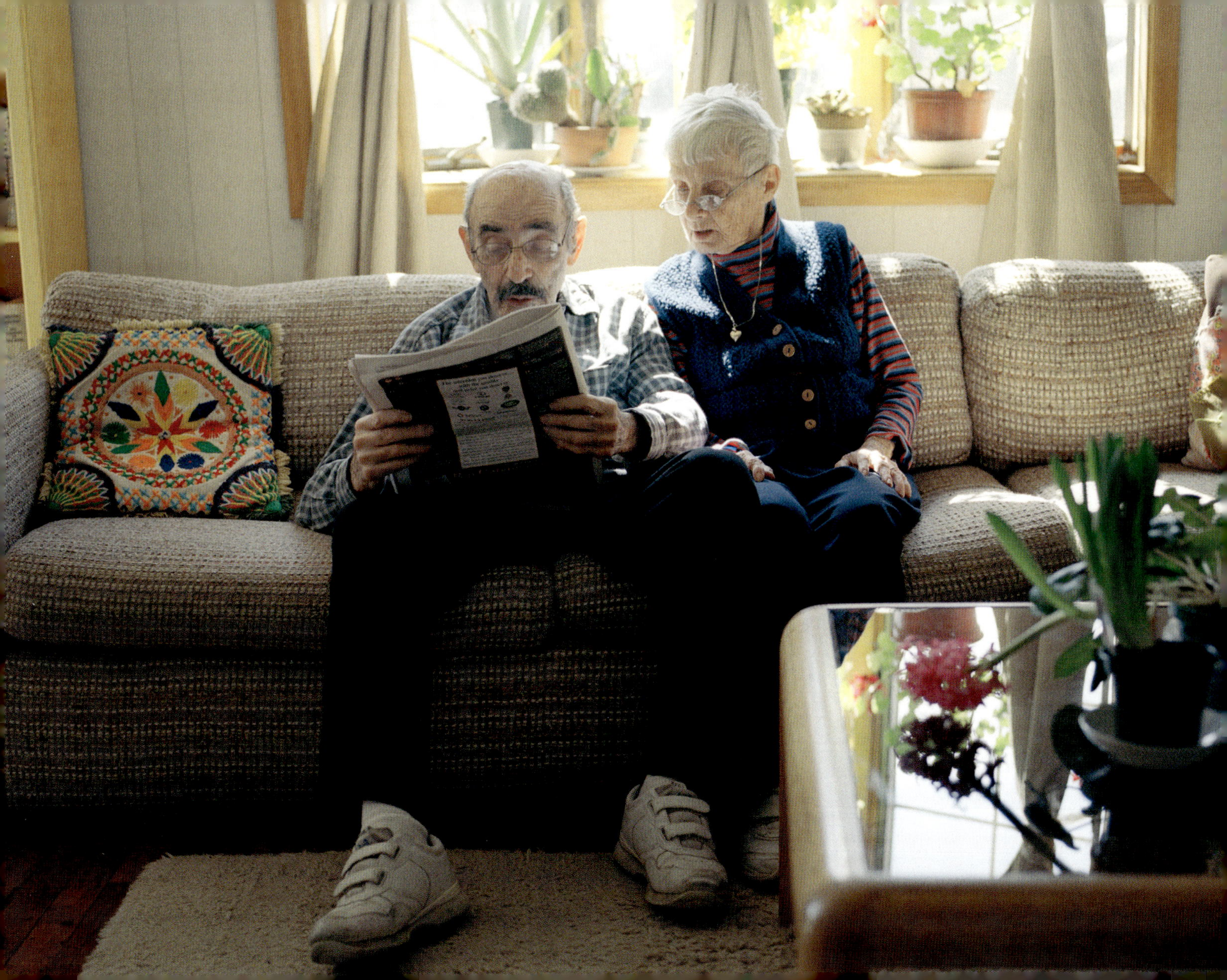

## Irving and Raye Warren

Great Neck, New York
Married on April 14, 1940



*Raye* People ask me how long we're married, and I ask them, "Can you keep a secret?" And they say, "Sure." And I say, "So can I!" But then I give our age and the years we're married because it's almost like a badge. We are married 69 years, and I feel it's not enough. The days go by very quickly. As you get older, you kind of lean on each other more.

*Irv* Honey, if I leaned on you, you would fall right down on the floor.

We met when I lived in Brooklyn, and she lived in Jamaica, Queens. She claimed I was hanging around with four gangsters at the time, but we were all of 18 or 19 years old. We both liked to dance, and we still dance quite a bit.

At this dance, my friends and I had previously chipped in five dollars apiece, and we bought an old model T Ford. We had an arrangement that if we met someone that we liked, we would all take the young lady home. And I liked Raye when I met her. At the end of the evening, I went over to the fellows, and I said, "I met a young lady and I would like to take her home." And you know, we were knowledgeable young men at that time, and the other four guys looked at me and they asked me a very good question. They said, "Where is Jamaica?" And I said, "I don't know." So as a result they refused to take her home, and I had to go back and beg off taking her. I thought I would never see her again.

*Raye* There was something very gentle about Irv. He was a frustrated artist. He worked for a pharmaceutical firm, and in those days, when he was 18, he washed bottles and he swept floors. And when we got married, he married me for my money. I was making $15 a week, 12 hours a day, 6 days a week. And he was making $8. And the year that we went together we managed to put together a buck each so we'd have enough to get married. So that's exactly how it all started. We knew the Great Depression.

*Irv* I was attracted to her immediately. I thought she was one of the most beautiful girls I'd ever met. It was very strange, though—I had been going with another girl at the time so I was in between. Then I didn't see her for several months. And after those months something happened. I looked at Raye's picture, and I decided I would call her up.

And I'm sitting on her couch in the living room, and I can just picture it now. She walked in, she had on a cute fur hat

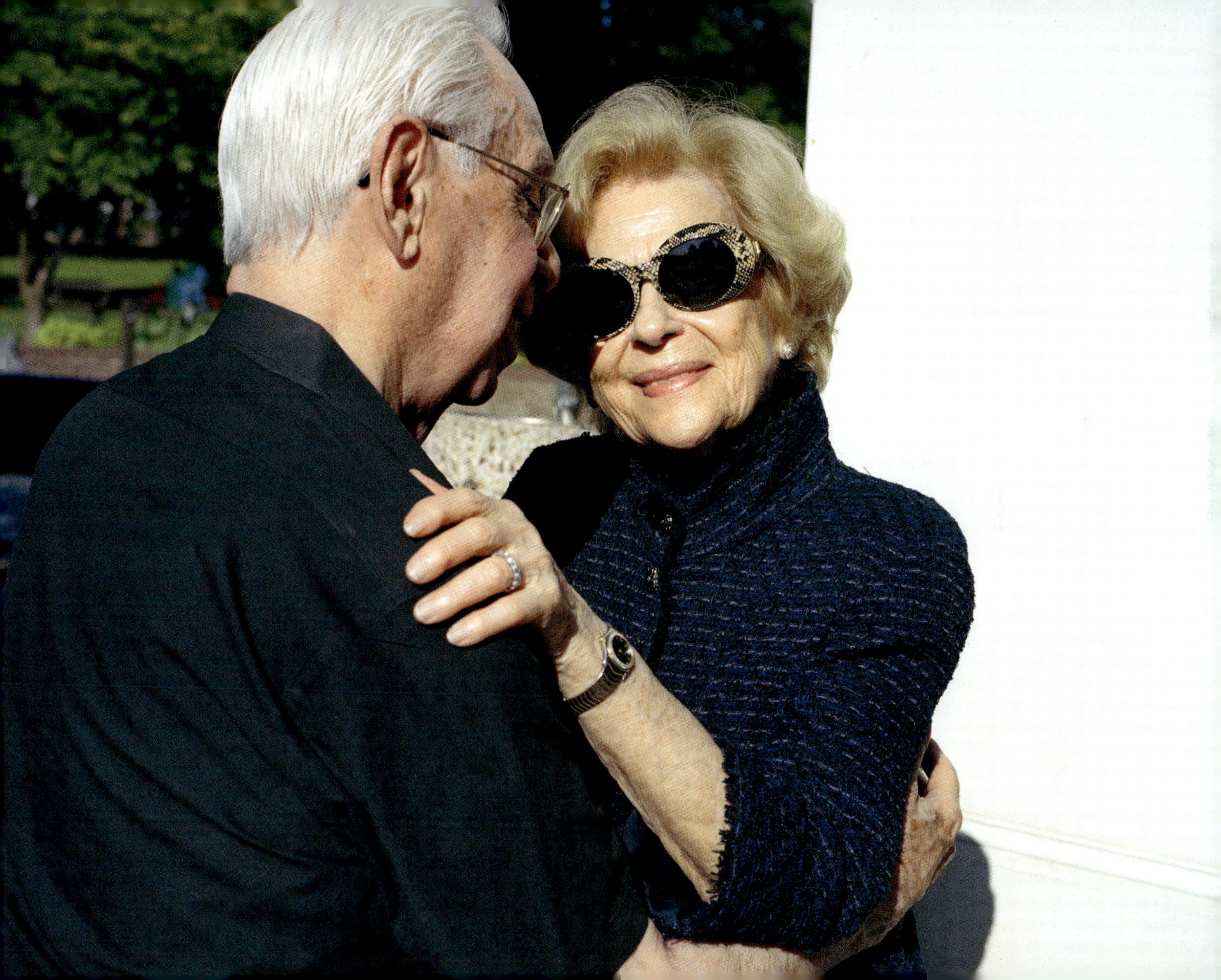

and short fur coat. And she walked in and I kept looking at her and she was looking at me and I walked up to her, turned my back and bent down and said, "Give me a swift kick in the behind!" You know, for not seeing her for nine months. But that was the start of going together.

In my opinion, when two people meet, they are way apart. Then somewhere along the line, they have to come together. When I first went out with Raye, she was talking politics, and I had no idea what she was talking about because I was never exposed to politics. So would you believe I read Karl Marx's book, which is about 14,000 pages, just so I could discuss it with her? I tried to fit into her life, and she tried to fit into mine.



And I admired her, her knowledge, her strength. She was always there for me, and I always tried to be there for her. For a long period of time, I used to be shocked every time I would meet her. She always tried to please me. One week she made her own hat. The next week she made her own dress. It got to a point where I didn't know who I was going to meet the following week because I looked forward to it all the time.

*Raye* You know, I didn't choose him because he looked like George Raft when he was young. George Raft had shoe-polished black hair, which Irv had. And when I met him, he had a misplaced eyebrow on his upper lip. I never kissed a fellow with a mustache, and I didn't like it. I have sensitive lips, and sometimes they break out. He eventually got rid of his mustache.

*Irv* I couldn't keep my hands off her when I first met her.

*Raye* And would you believe that I was still a virgin when we got married? Well, that's how I was brought up. I couldn't be otherwise.

*Irv* When we see doctors, or even when we see friends, if I walk into a room and she's not there, they say, "Where's Raye?" If she walks into a room, they will say, "Where's Irv?" We just go together. It's as simple as that.

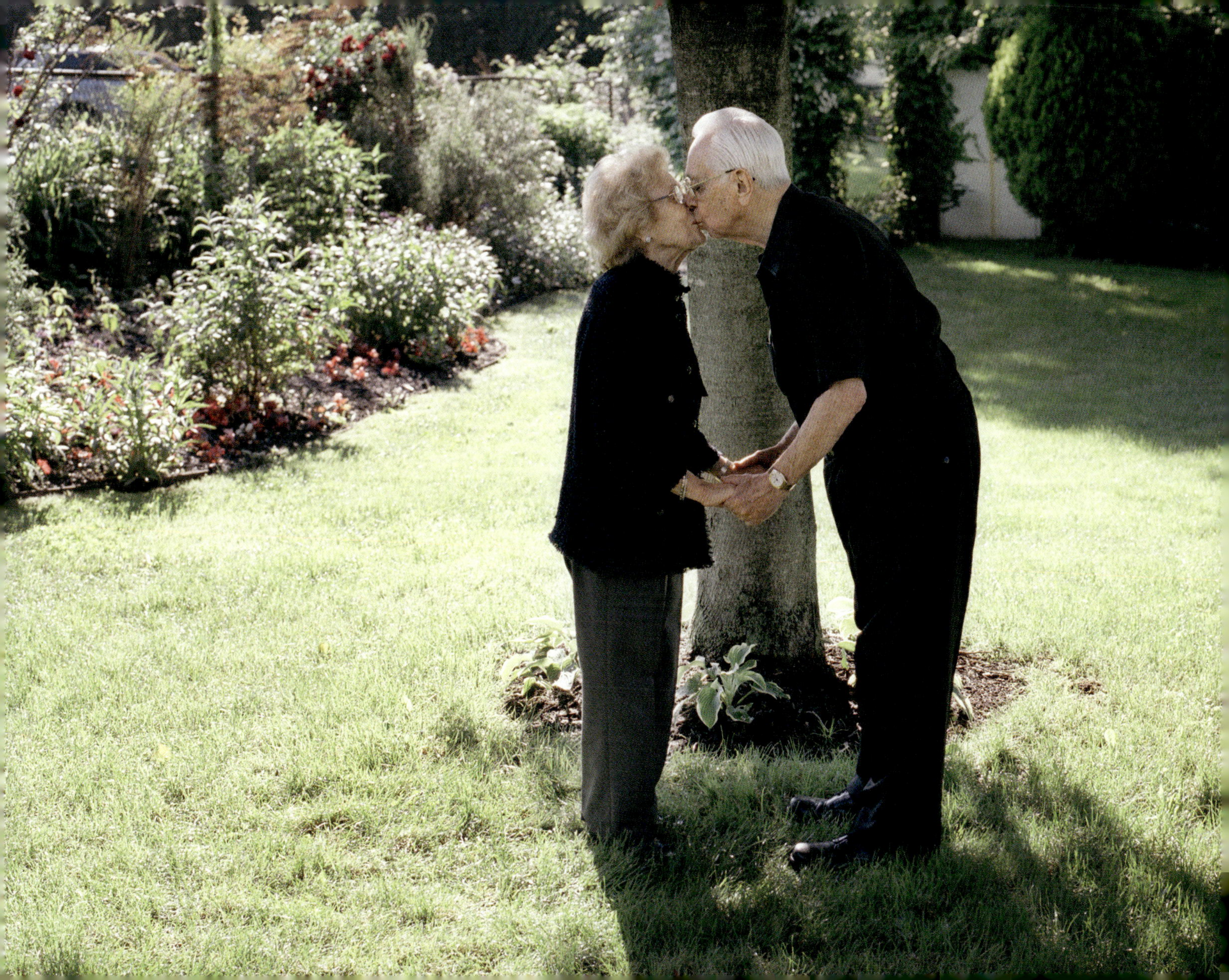

The greatest thanks to my brother Craig Fleishman for the camera I used to make this project. Thank you to Jeanne Lambert for the days and months she dedicated to proofing these texts and for her invaluable advice and guidance. Special thanks to Paul Moakley for traveling thousands of miles to accompany me in Pennsylvania, Oregon, Idaho and Wyoming.

And a special thank you to all of the couples who invited me into their homes and who shared their love stories.

ACKNOWLEDGMENTS

Jannik Anker, Can Başkent, Güngör Başkent, Aurelien Breeden, Yoni Brook, Nicole Caldwell, Camera Club of New York, Bryan Chang, Tom Cohen, Lucy Conticello, Maria Conticello, Marshall Cordell, Naomi Davis, Colin Dow, Bea Dreier, Michael Ebert, Judy Evans, Maria Filiozzi, Allen and Nancy Fleishman, Gerard Franciosa, Ellen Gold, Jose and Natalie Gomez, Jennifer Chau-Gong, Yumi Goto, Hélène Guilhot, Susanna Haglund, Donna Hale, Karen Bleyl Heck, Sol and Gloria Holtzman, Lyman and Susan Hurd, Michael Kissin, Lisa Krinsky, Karen Sweeney-Lemus, Reed and Terri Lesuma, Rose Leung, Victor Levie, Carrie Levy, Lydia Liao, Bob Linscott, Icy Liu, Christine Maes, Marty Markowitz, David and Maryia, Duarte Nunes, Dirk Pauwels, Vivian Pei, Chris and Pim, Gina Pinna, Melody Platz, Kira Pollack, Ingrid Posniack, James Reilley, Tony Rhodes, Julie Rizzo, Abby Robinson, Cliff Robinson, Elias Roman, Lily Rothman, Brett Rudd, Carl Rutberg, Kathy Ryan, Mark Rykoff, Fatima Salaria, Mark and Alison Savin, Maarten and Maria Louise Schilt, Silke and Sebastian, Ronen Segall, Taryn Simon, Juliana Sohn, Moon Ja Sohn, Bambi Salem de'Spagnolis, Marisa de'Spagnolis, Luigi Stamegna, Amber Terranova, Petang Unlimited, Alison Unterreiner, Norma Vogelman, Dennis de Vries, Jane Butkin Wagner, Vaughn Wallace, Sherry Warren, Tony Frosty Welch, Mark Zustovich

ISBN 978 90 5330 836 3


COPY EDITOR Jeanne Lambert

TRANSLATIONS Can Başkent, Aurelien Breeden, Hélène Guilhot, David Kwak, Bambi Salem de' Spagnolis, AnRong Xu

DESIGN Victor Levie | MV LevievanderMeer, Amsterdam
www.levievandermeer.nl

TEXT CORRECTION Kumar Jamdagni, Zwolle, www.language-matters.nl

IMAGE PROCESSING Gerard Franciosa and My Own Color Lab, NYC

PRINT & LOGISTICS MANAGEMENT KOMESO GmbH, Stuttgart
www.komeso.com

PRINTING Offizin Scheufele, Stuttgart, www.scheufele.de

DISTRIBUTION IN NORTH AMERICA Ingram Publisher Services
One Ingram Blvd., LaVergne, TN 37086, IPS: 866-765-0179
Email: customer.service@ingrampublisherservices.com

DISTRIBUTION IN THE NETHERLANDS AND FLANDERS Centraal Boekhuis

DISTRIBUTION IN ALL OTHER COUNTRIES Thames & Hudson Ltd
181a High Holborn, London WC1 V 7QX
Phone: +44 (0) 20 7845 5000
Fax: +44 (0) 20 7845 5055, e-mail: sales@thameshudson.co.uk

Schilt Publishing books, limited editions and prints
are available online via www.schiltpublishing.com
*Enquiries via sales@schiltpublishing.com*